D1532091

Women in Sport

SPORTS, GAMES, AND PASTIMES INFORMATION GUIDE SERIES

Series Editor: Ronald M. Ziegler, Humanities Reference Librarian, Holland Reference Library, Washington State University, Pullman

Also in this series:

BICYCLES AND BICYCLING—*Edited by Barbara A. Schultz and Mark P. Schultz*

CAMPING AND BACKPACKING—*Edited by Cecil F. Clotfelter and Mary L. Clotfelter*

GAMBLING—*Edited by Jack I. Gardner*

GOLF—*Edited by Joseph S.F. Murdoch and Janet Seagle*

HORSEMANSHIP—*Edited by Ellen B. Wells*

MOTORSPORTS—*Edited by Susan Ebershoff-Coles and Charla Ann Leibenguth*

PRIVATE AVIATION—*Edited by Floyd Nester Reister*

RACKET AND PADDLE GAMES—*Edited by David Peele**

WILDERNESS WATERWAYS—*Edited by Ronald M. Ziegler*

*in preparation

The above series is part of the
GALE INFORMATION GUIDE LIBRARY

The Library consists of a number of separate series of guides covering major areas in the social sciences, humanities, and current affairs.

General Editor: Paul Wasserman, Professor and former Dean, School of Library and Information Services, University of Maryland

Managing Editor: Denise Allard Adzigian, Gale Research Company

Women in Sport

A GUIDE TO INFORMATION SOURCES

Volume 10 in the Sports, Games, and Pastimes Information Guide Series

Mary L. Remley

Associate Professor
Indiana University
Bloomington

Gale Research Company
Book Tower, Detroit, Michigan 48226

Library of Congress Cataloging in Publication Data

Remley, Mary L
    Women in Sport.

    (Sports, games, and pastimes information guide
series ; v. 10) (Gale information guide library)
    Includes indexes.
    1. Sports for women—Bibliography. 2. Women
athletes—Biography—Bibliography. 3. Sports for
women—Information services. 4. Women athletes—
Biography—Information services. I. Title.
II. Series.
Z7963.S6R45 [GV709] 796'.01'94 [B] 80-14773
ISBN 0-8103-1461-4

To
Judy, Winifred, Cate and Ole
for their special support of
my professional endeavors

VITA

Mary L. Remley is presently associate professor at Indiana University, Bloomington. She received her B.S. Ed. from Southeast Missouri State, her M. Ed. from Ohio University, and her Ph.D. from University of Southern California.

Remley is president of the North American Society for Sports History and belongs to other sports and physical education affiliated organizations. She has written articles on sports for several journals in addition to giving presentations at universities and conferences.

CONTENTS

Contents

SERIES EDITOR'S PREFACE

This book is the tenth in the Sports, Games, and Pastimes Information Guide Series. The series embraces a diversity of literature on leisure activities. It may be axiomatic that when an individual is attracted to a sport or pastime, he or she longs to learn more about it, making a fertile spawning bed for specialized publications on the subject. Such publication possibilities do not languish unnoticed for long.

As a result, an announcement that there is a proliferation of sports and recreation literature hardly qualifies as news. However, to those not associated with recreation research, subject-area collection building, and the publication of reference works in the field, it may be less obvious that there has not been a concurrent development in sports and recreation bibliography to accurately record this growth. This series of information guides represents an acknowledgment of the need for bibliographic control, and an attempt to impose that control through the identification of books and other information sources within a wide range of sports, games, and pastimes. Volumes in this series will attempt to provide librarians, researchers, practitioners, and others with selective annotated lists of books and other pertinent information.

While women have been active in sport throughout recorded time, it is only recently that the literature has reflected this activity to a significant extent. The decade just ending has witnessed the greatest upsurge in both participation and publication. WOMEN IN SPORT gives timely and comprehensive reference aid in accessing information within this already abundant and ever-expanding sports scene. In her work, Mary L. Remley has organized hundreds of books and other information sources into four main parts. Parts 1-3 comprise the annotated listings of books; part 4, the references to periodicals, films, conference reports, sports halls of fame, and other data. Professor Remley's expertise becomes clearly evident when reading the bibliographic annotations, which manage to adequately describe and evaluate the material while somehow remaining refreshingly succinct.

Preface

WOMEN IN SPORT satisfies a bibliographic need in an era of rapidly changing teaching, research and participant interest, and has the intrinsic qualities required to insure its speedy acceptance as a basic reference source.

Ronald Ziegler, Series Editor
Washington State University

INTRODUCTION

Man's involvement in sport, games, and dance is as old as civilization. Throughout recorded history the athletic prowess of man has been extolled or excoriated, depending upon the esteem in which physical activity was held. Literature through the ages has discussed the role of sport, play, and games in the life of man. Rarely, however, has much attention been given to the place of such activities in the life of woman.

The recent surge of interest in the burgeoning sports programs for girls and women appears to be a modern phenomenon. In reality, however, woman's involvement in sporting activities has a heritage as old as civilization. Ancient Egyptian woman played ball and performed acrobatics; the Spartan woman of the fifth and sixth centuries B.C. had her own version of the Olympic Games; medieval woman danced, hunted, and learned to "carry the falcon gracefully." In the United States women have participated in sports and games from the time the first colonies were established. Colonial woman had her foot races; late nineteenth-century woman emerged as the bloomer girl, bicyclist, and basketball enthusiast; and the woman of the twentieth century may be found in the gym, on the field, and on the court, playing all kinds of games, the usual and the unusual.

Resources that provide insight into woman's participation in physical activities are sparse and scattered, often no more than a paragraph buried in discussions of the education of woman; a brief entry in the daily diary of an early colonist; or a periodical article extolling the virtues of exercise for woman. In the last ten years the literature pertaining to woman and sport has increased immensely. Periodicals specializing in the subject have been published; biographies of sports heroines have appeared, of both contemporary heroines and the early women who defied society's dictates and excelled in an essentially masculine endeavor. Instructional techniques specifically for the female in sport have been written. Sports halls of fame have included sportswomen among their members, and special conferences have been held to discuss the myriad aspects of the woman in sport.

In spite of such an increase in interest in woman and sport, a dearth of information still exists. This book was an attempt to determine just what kinds of material did exist and to collect and annotate as much as possible. The infor-

Introduction

mation should be useful to a variety of individuals who may be involved with women and sport--the teacher, researcher, coach, administrator, and the person most intimately involved in the area, the sportswoman herself. Perhaps it may also serve as an inspiration for others to contribute to the literature on the subject and thus help fill the gaps that still exist.

Much of the information contained herein was developed from resources at the Library of Congress. Publishers, too, have been generous in helping to supply information, and many other individuals have made contributions to the book in a variety of ways. I would be remiss if I failed to recognize the many active sportswomen who have served as an inspiration for this undertaking and the students from my classes in "Women in Sport" who motivated me to seek out new information continually for sharing with them. A special thanks must go to my good friends for encouragement and support during the project, and to Ronald Ziegler, the series editor, for his patience and understanding.

Part I

GENERAL REFERENCE WORKS

Although women have been actively involved with sport for many years, the subject has not seemed to be of particular interest to sports writers. Very few books have been devoted to the history of women in sport, and general references specific to the subject are also scarce. In terms of history, however, material written in a particular time period can offer historical perspective for that era.

Chapter 1 includes books that provide information on the history of women's involvement with sport. Several early publications have been selected for inclusion since they can provide a general view of the status of women and sport at the time of publication. The few recent books that deal specifically with history of women's sports are included in the second section, and the final sections list books concerned with the Olympic Games. Chapter 2 contains books that offer general information about women and sport in a variety of different subject areas. Chapter 3 suggests a basic list of recommended books.

Throughout this book selections may appear that are not devoted exclusively to women and sport. The decision to include such books was based on the kind of information contained in them, very often information not available from other sources.

Chapter 1

HISTORICAL WORKS

SELECTED EARLY PUBLICATIONS OF HISTORICAL INTEREST

Berenson, Senda, ed. LINE BASKET BALL OR BASKET BALL FOR WOMEN.
New York: American Sports Publishing Co., 1901. 50 p. Paperbound.

As the first published rules for women's basketball, this book continues to have historical significance. An editorial by Berenson describes the background for the development of the rules, and articles on the psychological and physiological effects of basketball on women provide insight into the game for women at the turn of the century. Official rules for playing the game are detailed, and Berenson's article, "The Significance of Basket Ball for Women," provides an excellent view of the sport for women at that time, as well as her prevailing philosophy about the sport.

Bolton, Florence. EXERCISES FOR WOMEN. New York: Funk and Wagnalls Co., 1914. 141 p.

Although this book is primarily concerned with calisthenics for women, it contains information which is related to attitudes about physical activity for women at the time. In a chapter titled "Clothes an Important Factor," the author discusses in great detail the kind of clothes appropriate for activity, covering everything from corset to shoes. Such topics as the bath in relation to exercise and the proper time for exercise are presented in another section. A series of exercises for women is described and illustrated in concluding chapters.

Dudley, Gertrude, and Kellor, Frances A. ATHLETIC GAMES IN THE EDUCATION OF WOMEN. New York: Henry Holt and Co., 1909. 268 p.

This book was written to clarify the educational values of team sports for women. Based on information from questionnaires sent to high schools and colleges, the book provides a general feeling for the prevailing philosophy about such activities for women. In addition to values of athletic games, the authors also describe the "present conditions" of competitive games in high schools, colleges, and organizations. A concluding section provides instructional techniques and general suggestions for teaching basketball, indoor baseball, and field hockey to women.

Duncan, Margaret M., and Cundiff, Velda P. PLAY DAYS FOR GIRLS AND WOMEN. New York: A.S. Barnes and Co., 1929. 87 p.

The play day developed in the 1920s as a "type of athletic competition . . . which is socially sound as well as physically wholesome" (p. v). This book describes in detail the nature of the play day for girls which was offered as a substitute for the more highly competitive programs under scrutiny at the time. Emphasis is placed on participation by everyone, and the book outlines all the information necessary for planning and conducting the play day from that philosophical viewpoint.

Hill, Lucille Eaton. ATHLETIC AND OUT-DOOR SPORTS FOR WOMEN. New York: Macmillan Co., 1903. 339 p.

This book was one of the earliest publications in the United States devoted exclusively to women's sports. Several different authors contributed to the book with descriptions of a variety of activities for women including basketball, hockey, golf, tennis, rowing, track athletics, horseback riding, and cross-country walking. Hill's introduction to the book provides an enlightened view of the value of sports for women in the early 1900s. Of particular interest are the illustrations of women in each of the activities, which provide their own kind of history for this period of development in women's sports.

National Amateur Athletic Federation. Women's Division, eds. WOMEN AND ATHLETICS. New York: A.S. Barnes and Co., 1930. 95 p. Paperbound.

A collection of nineteen papers dealing with diverse topics related to women's athletics was compiled for this book. Such provocative titles as "Safeguarding Girls' Athletics," "Are State Championships Educationally Sound?" and "The Playtime of a Million Girls or an Olympic Victory--Which?" are suggestive of the prevailing attitudes about athletics for women. The book also includes a description of the activities, aims, and "platform" of beliefs of the Women's Division, National Amateur Athletic Federation, which was founded in 1923 and exerted considerable influence on women's sports for almost twenty years.

Paret, J. Parmly. THE WOMAN'S BOOK OF SPORT. New York: D. Appleton and Co., 1901. 167 p.

This book, another of the earliest devoted exclusively to women, was written as an instructional manual on sports for women and includes information on golf, tennis, sailing a catboat, swimming, bicycling, and basketball. A separate chapter offers advice on exercises for healthful physical development, and a final section provides information about men's sports so women can be intelligent spectators at such events. The turn-of-the-century flavor of women's sports is captured in the photographs of women participants.

Sefton, Alice Allene. THE WOMEN'S DIVISION, NATIONAL AMATEUR ATHLETIC FEDERATION: SIXTEEN YEARS OF PROGRESS IN ATHLETICS FOR GIRLS AND WOMEN, 1923-1939. Stanford, Calif.: Stanford University Press, 1941. 88 p.

This book describes the general philosophy and historical development of the Women's Division and its promotion of wholesome sports for women. The aims of the division are detailed in twelve essays written by women who were leaders in the organization. One section is devoted to the procedural aspects of the division and to the kinds of work the group performed such as conferences, research, field work, and publications. In a section titled "The Future," the philosophy of girl's and women's sports promulgated by the division at this time is clearly stated. The book provides an excellent view of sports for women which was supported by many individuals and organizations in the 1920s and 1930s.

Somers, Florence A. PRINCIPLES OF WOMEN'S ATHLETICS. New York: A.S. Barnes and Co., 1930. 151 p.

This book was designed to provide basic principles for the selection and conduct of athletic programs for girls and women. The author discusses factors related to women's participation, current trends in participation and competition, and conditions that have influenced the development of sports for women. A list of principles for the development of women's programs is presented with supporting and clarifying commentary for each statement. A general feeling that the author is dealing with a "problem"--women's athletics--pervades the book; however, it provides insight into the attitudes toward women's involvement in sport that prevailed in this time period.

THE SPORTSWOMAN. Vols. 1-10. Bryn Mawr, Pa.: Constance M.K. Applebee, 1925-33. Monthly, except July and August.

This magazine originated as the official organ of the United States Field Hockey Association, but from the outset carried articles about other sports activities. It was the only regularly published periodical devoted exclusively to women's sports and the issues contain a wealth of historical information about women's activities in the years of publication. Field hockey continued to be a major focus of many articles; however, many other sports in which women were involved were featured in each issue.

HISTORIES OF WOMEN'S SPORTS

Flint, Rachael Heyhoe, and Rheinberg, Netta. FAIR PLAY, THE STORY OF WOMEN'S CRICKET. London: Angus and Robertson Publishers, 1976. 192 p.

In this book about an unusual sport for women, the authors trace the history of cricket from the 1700s to the present time. Separate sections are devoted to the development of the sport in countries outside the British Isles. One of the chapters covers major women players in the sport in the past fifty years. Excellent photographs illustrate the book; particularly notable are those of players in the late 1800s.

Lichtenstein, Grace. A LONG WAY, BABY. New York: William Morrow and Co., 1974. 239 p.

Newspaper reporter and author Lichtenstein reviews the 1973 women's tennis circuit through reports of selected tournaments. She provides some personal glimpses of the "tennis" lives of well-known players and brief insights into the growth of women's professional tennis.

Ramsden, Caroline. LADIES IN RACING, SIXTEENTH CENTURY TO THE PRESENT DAY. London: Stanley Paul and Co., 1973. 192 p.

Rather than being a definitive history of British women's involvement in horse racing, this book highlights several different dimensions of that involvement. Chapters briefly review women owners, trainers, bookmakers, racing journalists and jockeys. Some reference is made to women riders in the 1700s and 1800s, but most of the book deals with horsewomen of the twentieth century.

Schickel, Richard. THE WORLD OF TENNIS. New York: Random House, 1975. 251 p.

One of the prime merits of this book is its excellent photographs. Although only one of the ten chapters is devoted wholly to women's tennis, Schickel has done a reasonable job of providing a historic overview of women's play. He begins, however, with Suzanne Lenglen and thus omits some of the earlier pioneer champions of women's tennis.

Tingay, Lance. TENNIS: A PICTORIAL HISTORY. Rev. ed. London: William Collins Sons and Co., 1979. 168 p.

The title of this book aptly describes its content; it is filled with excellent photographs dating from the 1870s, and additional drawings illustrate the early history of tennis. Ample narrative provides an overview of the development of the sport in chronologically organized sections from "The Genesis of a Sport," to "Tennis as Big Business." Approximately half of the photographs are of women, and of special note are those of very early champions which are not readily available in other sources: Lotte Dod, youngest Wimbledon champion; May Sutton, first overseas player to win Wimbledon; M. Coles, playing in straw hat and long skirt in 1910; and the energetic antics of Suzanne Lenglen in the 1920s. A list of winners of all major championships beginning with Wimbledon in 1877 concludes the book.

THE OLYMPIC GAMES

Kieran, John; Daley, Arthur; and Jordan, Pat. THE STORY OF THE OLYMPIC GAMES, 776 B.C. TO 1976. Philadelphia: J.B. Lippincott Co., 1976. 575 p.

This "story" of the Olympic Games tells only a partial story. Until the discussion of the 1948 games, women's accomplishments are omitted. Comments prior to that are limited to women's exclusion from the Olympic Village in Los Angeles in 1932, Eleanor Holm's removal from the U.S. team for drinking champagne aboard ship enroute to the 1936 games, and the notation that women participated in track and field events for the first time in 1928. Coverage for women's events improves somewhat in the accounts following the 1948 games, and the accomplishments of women in the more recent games are far more detailed. Gold medal winners of all events for women and men and locations of the games since 1896 are listed.

Killanin, Lord, and Rodda, John, eds. THE OLYMPIC GAMES: EIGHTY YEARS OF PEOPLE AND EVENTS. London: Barrie and Jenkins, 1976. 272 p.

The major focus of this book is on the Olympic participants and their events from the time of the first modern games in 1896. Separate sections describe highlights in each Olympiad, both winter and summer, and the accomplishments of women are included from their first appearance in the games in 1900. Brief histories of each Olympic event also note the participation of women. "Who's Who in the Olympic Games" provides brief biographical data for outstanding Olympic champions, and several women are included. Many of the excellent photographs illustrating the book are of women.

Simri, Uriel. A HISTORICAL ANALYSIS OF THE ROLE OF WOMEN IN THE MODERN OLYMPIC GAMES. Wingate Monograph Series no. 1. Netanya, Israel: Wingate Institute for Physical Education and Sport, Netanya, 1977. 50 p. Paperbound.

Simri provides a brief history of women's involvement in the Olympic Games and identifies the changing nature of the activities in which women participate. He is adamant in noting errors about women in the games made by other authors, but though he points out their mistakes, he does not always provide his own reliable source. In addition to the historical analysis of women in the games, Simri also discusses the growth in participation by women and the current status of their involvement.

SELECTED BOOKS WITH LIMITED COVERAGE OF WOMEN IN THE OLYMPIC GAMES

Benagh, Jim. INCREDIBLE OLYMPIC FEATS. New York: McGraw-Hill Book Co., 1976. 178 p. Paperbound.

Chester, David. THE OLYMPIC GAMES HANDBOOK. New York: Charles Scribner's Sons, 1975. 268 p.

Durant, John. HIGHLIGHTS OF THE OLYMPICS. 5th ed. New York: Hastings House Publishers, 1977. 240 p.

Henry, Bill. AN APPROVED HISTORY OF THE OLYMPIC GAMES. New York: G.P. Putnam's Sons, 1976. 415 p.

Schaap, Dick. AN ILLUSTRATED HISTORY OF THE OLYMPICS. New York: Alfred A. Knopf, 1978. 388 p.

Chapter 2
GENERAL REFERENCES

REFERENCES SPECIFIC TO WOMEN AND SPORT

Adrian, Marlene, and Brame, Judy, eds. NAGWS RESEARCH REPORTS. Vol. 3. Washington, D.C.: American Alliance for Health, Physical Education, and Recreation, 1977. 183 p. Paperbound.

> One of a series of research reports on women in sport, this volume emphasizes the female athlete. Several authors report on specific research projects using female athletes as subjects, and other articles suggest techniques which may be appropriate for conducting research on female sports participants. Hall includes an excellent bibliography on sociological aspects in her article, "The Sociological Perspective of Females in Sport." This volume is more aptly titled "Research Reports" than the two previous volumes since many of the selections are reports of research on female athletes rather than reviews of completed research.

Boslooper, Thomas, and Hayes, Marcia. THE FEMINITY GAME. New York: Stein and Day, 1974. 227 p.

> In this book the authors analyze societal expectations of the female, particularly in relation to the development of athletic skill. Physiological and psychological biases that have deterred women from entering the world of sport or pursuing success as a sportswoman after a certain age are discussed. Suggestions are offered to overcome prevailing biases, and some of the progress that has been made in providing opportunities in sport participation for women is briefly reviewed.

Dunkle, Margaret. COMPETITIVE ATHLETICS: IN SEARCH OF EQUAL OPPORTUNITY. Washington, D.C.: U.S. Department of Health, Education, and Welfare, 1976. 142 p. Paperbound.

> This manual was designed to provide technical assistance to agencies and institutions to ensure compliance with Title IX of the Education Amendments of 1972. It was prepared for use primarily by athletic directors, administrators, and coaches to eliminate sex discrimina-

tion in athletic programs. Some general information concerning equal opportunity in athletic programs is followed by chapters on specific aspects of compliance with Title IX. Model assessment tools are provided for use in evaluating each of several areas of concern. A bibliography of selected resources concerned with equity concludes the manual.

Geadelmann, Patricia; Grant, Christine; Slatton, Yvonne; and Burke, N. Peggy. EQUALITY IN SPORTS FOR WOMEN. Washington, D.C.: American Alliance for Health, Physical Education, and Recreation, 1977. 202 p. Paperbound.

This book was designed as a manual to provide the tools for eliminating sex-biased discrimination and inequality in sports. A broad range of information is covered and includes the following: clarification of federal regulations relating to equity; ways and places to file a complaint if inequity is believed to exist; nationally organized women's groups and civil rights and professional groups, whose work focuses on equality of opportunity; a summary of fifteen court cases on sex discrimination in athletics; and procedures for effecting change when inequities exist. A detailed appendix of basic information for dealing with inequities and a long list of references further enhance this collection of tools for effecting change in sports programs.

Gerber, Ellen W.; Felshin, Jan; Berlin, Pearl; and Wyrick, Waneen. THE AMERICAN WOMAN IN SPORT. Reading, Mass.: Addison-Wesley Publishing Co., 1974. 562 p.

The four authors of this text have combined their expertise to provide an analysis of the American woman in sport, but have limited their information to females of college age or older. Each writer has explored the role of woman in sport within specific boundaries: the historical development of sport for women; the sportswoman in the context of society; psychological dimensions of the woman in sport; and the biophysical factors of the female as they relate to her participation in sport. Each section is concluded with an extensive bibliography.

Harris, Dorothy V. DGWS RESEARCH REPORTS: WOMEN IN SPORT. Vol. 1. Washington, D.C.: American Association for Health, Physical Education, and Recreation, 1971. 104 p. Paperbound.

The title of this volume may be misleading as the collection of articles by fifteen different authors presents syntheses of completed research on the female sports participant rather than reports of results of individual studies by the writers. Excellent bibliographies accompany most of the articles, however, and information is included on the psychosocial, physiological, and teaching-coaching aspects of women in sport.

_____. DGWS RESEARCH REPORTS: WOMEN IN SPORT. Vol. 2. Washington, D.C.: American Association for Health, Physical Education, and Recreation, 1973. 145 p. Paperbound.

This volume presents a collection of articles synthesizing recent research on women in sport. Information is included on the biomechanical, physiological, and psychological aspects of the female sports participant with good bibliographies accompanying most of the articles.

Hoepner, Barbara J., ed. WOMEN'S ATHLETICS: COPING WITH CONTROVERSY. Washington, D.C.: American Association for Health, Physical Education, and Recreation, 1974. 120 p. Paperbound.

The presentations of fourteen speakers who dealt with the topic, "Women's Athletics," at the 1973 convention of the American Association for Health, Physical Education, and Recreation are included in this monograph, along with two other presentations from the 1973 National Coaches Conference of the Division for Girls' and Women's Sports. The papers are organized under the following headings: "Overview Women's Rights"; "Women's Intercollegiate Athletics Past, Present, Future"; "The Olympic Games"; "Women in Athletics"; and "Welfare of Women in Sports." The speakers represent a broad range of interests from teachers, researchers, and administrators to coaches and Olympic athletes, and the papers are a reflection of the diverse views of such a group.

Kaplan, Janice. WOMEN AND SPORTS: INSPIRATION AND INFORMATION FOR THE NEW FEMALE ATHLETE. New York: Viking Press, 1979. 204 p.

Utilizing a writing style for the general reader, the author of this book provides an interesting overview of the current sport scene for women. She covers a variety of topics including physiological aspects of sport for women, nutrition, selecting one's sport, and competition. She promotes integrated sports for men and women whenever possible, but is particularly concerned that women's sports of the future not be modeled after the programs of men's sports.

Klafs, Carl E., and Lyon, M. Joan. THE FEMALE ATHLETE. 2d ed. St. Louis: C.V. Mosby, 1978. 341 p. Paperbound.

Although the focus of this book is on conditioning as a means of preventing injury, information in a variety of areas is included. A brief history of woman's participation in sports introduces the book, and remaining sections cover anthropometric and physiological factors in sport performance; physical conditioning; and sports training which is primarily concerned with care and prevention of injuries. Chapters are included in the last section, however, on nutrition and athletic performance and the facts and fallacies pertaining to ergogenic aids. A special feature of the book is the inclusion of individual training programs of several champion athletes in a variety of sports.

Oglesby, Carole A. WOMEN AND SPORT: FROM MYTH TO REALITY. Philadelphia: Lea and Febiger, 1978. 256 p. Paperbound.

The author describes this series of papers by several different authors, all women, as a book about sports feminism. It is, however, a provocative collection of material that explores a variety of subjects concerned with the female and sport. A brief history of women's participation in sport introduces the book and is followed by thirteen chapters set in the framework of sections titled "Society and the Female Body"; "Society, Sport, and Sexuality"; "Society, Sport Involvement, and Sport Achievement"; and "Women's Sport: Myth, Reality, and Social Change." Most chapters have detailed bibliographies. While the book may appear to be strongly slanted toward the feminist viewpoint, the authors have provided an excellent collection of theoretical and practical information about the problems and the positive aspects that evolve from women's sports participation.

Price, La Ferne Ellis. THE WONDER OF MOTION: A SENSE OF LIFE FOR WOMEN. Grand Forks: University of North Dakota Press, 1970. 79 p.

This book is an attempt to explore the emotional element of woman's involvement in sport. Both verbal images in the form of free verse and artistic illustrations are used to portray women in a variety of sports. The book is essentially one of introspection-- an effort to describe the inner feelings of the female as she engages in sporting activities.

Spirduso, Waneen Wyrick, ed. BIBLIOGRAPHY OF RESEARCH INVOLVING FEMALE SUBJECTS. Washington, D.C.: American Alliance for Health, Physical Education, and Recreation, 1974. 212 p. Paperbound.

This monograph is a compilation of titles of theses and dissertations from ninety-three institutions in which women were the subject of the study. The author, title, year, and institution are provided for the studies, which are organized under the following categories: motor learning; sport psychology; physiological aspects of motor performance; sport studies; physical education for the handicapped; health; teaching methods, curriculum, and administration; and recreation and leisure.

Twin, Stephanie L. OUT OF THE BLEACHERS. Old Westbury, N.Y.: Feminist Press, 1979. 229 p. Paperbound.

Twin introduces this anthology with a brief history of woman's involvement in sport and the societal views of woman's role that have curtailed her participation. The articles that follow explore the place of woman in the sports world through both contemporary and historical writings. Separate sections are devoted to physiological aspects and social attitudes; reflections on the lives of selected sportswomen; and the structure of women's sports. While some readers may question the selection of articles for inclusion in the book, the author is to be commended for her contribution to an area in which the literature is still so sparse.

SELECTIONS WITH CHAPTERS OR SECTIONS ON WOMEN AND SPORT

Beisser, Arnold R. THE MADNESS IN SPORTS. 2d ed. Bowie, Md.: Charles Press Publishers, 1977. 207 p. Paperbound.

Butt, Dorcas. PSYCHOLOGY OF SPORT. New York: Van Nostrand Reinhold Co., 1976. 196 p. Paperbound.

Clerici, Gianni. THE ULTIMATE TENNIS BOOK: 500 YEARS OF THE SPORT. Chicago: Follette Publishing Co., 1975. 355 p.

Coakley, Jay J. SPORT IN SOCIETY. St. Louis: C.V. Mosby, 1978. 349 p. Paperbound.

Eitzen, D. Stanley, and Sage, George H. SOCIOLOGY OF AMERICAN SPORT. Dubuque, Iowa: William C. Brown Co., 1978. 337 p.

Frost, Reuben B. ENCYCLOPEDIA OF PHYSICAL EDUCATION, FITNESS, AND SPORTS. Reading, Mass.: Addison-Wesley Publishing Co., 1977. 973 p.

Harris, Dorothy V. INVOLVEMENT IN SPORT: A SOMATOPSYCHIC RATIONALE FOR PHYSICAL ACTIVITY. Philadelphia: Lea and Febiger, 1973. 250 p.

Hart, Marie. SPORT IN THE SOCIOCULTURAL PROCESS. 2d ed. Dubuque, Iowa: William C. Brown Co., 1976. 509 p. Paperbound.

Lucas, John A., and Smith, Ronald A. SAGA OF AMERICAN SPORT. Philadelphia: Lea and Febiger, 1978. 439 p.

Michener, James A. SPORTS IN AMERICA. New York: Random House, 1976. 466 p.

Miller, Donna Mae, and Russell, Kathryn R.E. SPORT: A CONTEMPORARY VIEW. Philadelphia: Lea and Febiger, 1971. 202 p.

Novak, Michael. THE JOY OF SPORTS. New York: Basic Books, 1976. 357 p. Paperbound.

Olan, Ben, ed. A CENTURY OF CHAMPIONS. New York: Macmillan Publishing Co., 1976. 256 p.

General References

Rooney, John F. A GEOGRAPHY OF AMERICAN SPORT. Reading, Mass.: Addison-Wesley Publishing Co., 1974. 306 p.

Spears, Betty, and Swanson, Richard. HISTORY OF SPORT AND PHYSICAL ACTIVITY IN THE UNITED STATES. Dubuque, Iowa: William C. Brown Co., 1978. 402 p.

Talamani, John T., and Page, Charles H. SPORT AND SOCIETY. Boston: Little, Brown and Co., 1973. 493 p. Paperbound.

Twombley, Wells. 200 YEARS OF SPORT IN AMERICA. New York: McGraw-Hill Book Co., 1976. 287 p.

Weiss, Paul. SPORT, A PHILOSOPHIC INQUIRY. Carbondale: Southern Illinois University Press, 1969. 274 p. Paperbound.

Willoughby, David P. THE SUPER ATHLETES. New York: A.S. Barnes and Co., 1970. 665 p.

Chapter 3
BASIC LIST OF RECOMMENDED BOOKS

The list of books that follows is an attempt to suggest a collection that provides a cross-section of information in the broad area of women in sport. Because of the diversity of information, the choice of titles was difficult and, of course, represents my own personal bias. With the exception of Hill's ATHLETIC AND OUT-DOOR SPORTS FOR WOMEN, most of the books should be currently available. I am hopeful that Hill's volume may soon be available in a reprint edition.

Two periodicals are included at the end of the book list, chosen for their coverage of general information on women in sport. The book selections are also of a more general nature. Persons with specific interests in either activities or biographies of personalities should consult the appropriate sections.

Davidson, Owen, and Jones, C.M. GREAT WOMEN TENNIS PLAYERS. London: Pelham Books, 1971. 142 p.

Elliot, Len, and Kelly, Barbara. WHO'S WHO IN GOLF. New Rochelle, N.Y.: Arlington House Publishers, 1976. 208 p.

Gerber, Ellen W.; Felshin, Jan; Berlin, Pearl; and Wyrick, Waneen. THE AMERICAN WOMAN IN SPORT. Reading, Mass.: Addison-Wesley Publishing Co., 1974. 562 p.

Haney, Lynn. THE LADY IS A JOCK. New York: Dodd, Mead and Co., 1973. 180 p.

Hill, Lucille Eaton. ATHLETIC AND OUT-DOOR SPORTS FOR WOMEN. New York: Macmillan Co., 1903. 339 p.

Hollander, Phyllis. 100 GREATEST WOMEN IN SPORTS. New York: Grosset and Dunlap, 1976. 142 p.

Jacobs, Helen Hull. GALLERY OF CHAMPIONS. Freeport, N.Y.: Books for Libraries, 1949, 1970. 224 p.

Recommended Books

Jacobs, Karen Folger. GIRLSPORTS. New York: Bantam Books, 1978. 180 p. Paperbound.

Johnson, William O., and Williamson, Nancy. WHATTA GAL! THE BABE DIDRIKSON STORY. Boston: Little, Brown, 1977. 224 p.

Jordan, Pat. BROKEN PATTERNS. New York: Dodd, Mead and Co., 1977. 213 p.

Kaplan, Janice. WOMEN AND SPORTS: INSPIRATION AND INFORMATION FOR THE NEW FEMALE ATHLETE. New York: Viking Press, 1979. 204 p.

Killanin, Lord, and Rodda, John, eds. THE OLYMPIC GAMES: EIGHTY YEARS OF PEOPLE AND EVENTS. London: Barrie and Jenkins, 1976. 272 p.

Klafs, Carl E., and Lyon, M. Joan. THE FEMALE ATHLETE. 2d ed. St. Louis: C.V. Mosby, 1978. 341 p. Paperbound.

Oglesby, Carole A. WOMEN AND SPORT: FROM MYTH TO REALITY. Philadelphia: Lea and Febiger, 1978. 256 p. Paperbound.

Sabin, Francene. WOMEN WHO WIN. New York: Random House, 1975. 171 p.

Stambler, Irwin. WOMEN IN SPORTS. Garden City, N.Y.: Doubleday and Co., 1975. 155 p.

Twin, Stephanie L. OUT OF THE BLEACHERS. Old Westbury, N.Y.: Feminist Press, 1979. 229 p. Paperbound.

Williams, Cicely. WOMEN ON THE ROPE. London: George Allen and Unwin, 1973. 240 p.

COACHING: WOMEN'S ATHLETICS. Wallingford, Conn.: Intercommunications, 1975-- . Bimonthly, except July and August.

WOMEN'S SPORTS. Palo Alto, Calif.: Women's Sports Publication, 1979-- . Monthly.

Part II

BIOGRAPHIES OF SPORTSWOMEN

For many years the sportswoman who excelled in her chosen activity went virtually unnoticed. She collected her trophies from national and local competitions and claimed her medals at the Olympic Games, but little written information detailed these accomplishments. The role expectation for the female did not include athletic achievement, and young girls who might aspire to such fame had few heroines for their models. In more recent years, however, society's view of the athletic female has tempered somewhat, and increasingly larger numbers of girls and women are found in the sports arena. In a short time the sports heroine has emerged, and her achievements have rather suddenly become of interest to others.

This section lists a number of books that detail the major events in the lives and sports careers of many prominent sportswomen. Chapter 4 includes volumes devoted exclusively to biographies of women or collections that include women among their selections. Books listed in chapter 5 are concerned with women who have excelled in specific sports. Biographical data may seem unnecessarily brief in some instances; however, the sports career of a Dorothy Hamill or a Tracy Austin has covered only a short time span. A surprising number of biographies have been written for young readers. These have been included in the selections, as they are indicative of the growing interest at all levels in the sports achievements of women.

Chapter 4

COLLECTIONS OF BIOGRAPHIES

Batten, Jack. CHAMPIONS. Toronto: New Press, 1971. 197 p.

The athletic accomplishments of several top sportswomen are detailed in this book of Canadian champions. Under such provocative chapter heads as "All Wet," "To Beat the Wind," "Grace on Ice," and "The Women of the Slopes," the feats of swimmers, track and field competitors, skaters, and skiers are described. Although both men and women are included in the book, a good portion is devoted to women, and some excellent photographs of women in action are included.

Berke, Art, ed. THE LINCOLN LIBRARY OF SPORTS CHAMPIONS. Vols. 11-14. Columbus, Ohio: Sports Resources Co., 1974. 191 p. each volume except vol. 14, 199 p.

This set of volumes was designed as a motivator to encourage reading at the elementary and secondary levels. In the selection of 500 sports champions for inclusion, forty-four of these are women. Biographical sketches focus on the contributions and significance of each individual in her sport, and excellent photographs illustrate special events in the lives of each champion. Women selected from various sports for the series follow, along with the volume number in which they appear. Badminton: Judy Devlin Hashman (6); baton twirling: Fran Pardey (10); bowling: Dotty Fothergill (4), Marion Ladewig (7); cycling: Sheila Young (14); diving: Pat McCormick (8), Katherine Rawls (10); horseback riding: Kathy Kusner (7); golf: Kathy Whitworth (13), Mickey Wright (14), Babe Didrikson Zaharias (14); gymnastics: Olga Korbut (7), Cathy Rigby (10); horse racing: Robyn Smith (12); riflery: Annie Oakley (9); rodeo: Terry Hearn (6); figure skating: Peggy Fleming (4), Sonja Henie (6), Janet Lynn (8); speed skating: Sheila Young (14); skiing: Barbara, Lindy, and Marilyn Cochran (3), Andrea Mead Lawrence (7); swimming: Florence Chadwick (3), Donna deVarona (4), Gertrude Ederle (4), Dawn Fraser (5), Shane Gould (5), Debbie Meyer (9), Katherine Rawls (10); tennis: Maureen Connolly (3), Margaret Court (3), Chris Evert (4), Althea Gibson (5), Evonne Goolagong (5), Helen Jacobs (6), Billie Jean King (7), Suzanne Lenglen (8), Alice

Marble (8), Helen Wills Moody (9); track and field: Fanny Blan-
kers-Koen (2), Wilma Rudolph (11), Babe Didrikson Zaharias (14);
volleyball: Nancy Owen (10); water skiing: Liz Allan Shetter
(11).

Borstein, Larry. AFTER OLYMPIC GLORY. New York: Frederick Warne and
Co., 1978. 185 p.

This book highlights the athletic careers of ten former Olympians,
four of whom are women: diver, Micki King; swimmer, Donna
deVarona; figure skater, Tenley Albright; and runner, Nell Jackson. Each biographical sketch focuses on the athletic careers of
the women and the focus of their lives following attainment of
Olympic success.

Campbell, Gail. MARATHON: THE WORLD OF THE LONG-DISTANCE ATH-
LETE. New York: Sterling Publishing Co., 1977. 176 p.

Several women are included in this book on distance running,
swimming and bicycling. Each of the three sections has an introduction with general information about the event, followed by
sketches of individuals who have competed and their major accomplishments. The largest number of women by far are the distance
swimmers. Included in that section are Gertrude Ederle, the first
woman to swim the English Channel, Florence Chadwick, Greta
Andersen, Lynne Cox, Diana Nyad, Marilyn Bell, and Marty Sinn.
No women cyclists are included; however, a chapter titled "The
Plight of the Female Runner" remarks on the early efforts of Kathy
Switzer and Roberta Bingay in the Boston Marathon.

Donovan, Hedley, ed. REMARKABLE AMERICAN WOMEN, 1776-1976. Life
Special Report. New York: Time, 1976. 116 p.

This special edition of LIFE magazine includes several athletes
selected, as noted by the editors, "either because of the notable
things they have done or the extraordinary lives they have led"
(p. 2). A brief paragraph noting some of their accomplishments
accompanies photographs of Tenley Albright, Gertrude Ederle,
Billie Jean King, Andrea Mead Lawrence, Wilma Rudolph, Eleonora
[sic] Sears, Helen Wills, and Babe Didrikson Zaharias.

Gemme, Leila [Boyle]. THE NEW BREED OF ATHLETE. New York: Pocket
Books, 1975. 190 p. Paperbound.

Of the twelve sports personalities selected for this book, two are
women. The author chose individuals who are generally considered
unconventional in the sports arena, and Kathy Kusner and Billie
Jean King fit her criteria. The biographical sketch of Kusner
describes her interests in horses and racing as an accomplished
Olympic equestrian and her battle with the Maryland State Racing
Commission to become the first woman jockey licensed to race on

the flat track. Major events in Billie Jean King's personal and professional life are highlighted in her biography. Particular attention is directed to her work in professional tennis and her efforts to gain equity for women.

Grimsley, Will, ed. THE SPORTS IMMORTALS. Englewood Cliffs, N.J.: Prentice-Hall, 1972. 320 p.

Of the fifty "greatest athletes in the history of modern sports" selected for inclusion in this book, only three are women. Biographies for Helen Wills Moody, Sonja Henie, and Babe Didrikson Zaharias sketch the highlights of their careers and provide an indication of why they are considered "sports immortals."

Gutman, Bill. MODERN WOMEN SUPERSTARS. New York: Dodd, Mead and Co., 1977. 112 p.

Gutman briefly sketches the sports careers of six women athletes who have excelled in their chosen sports. Biographical information is included for Chris Evert, tennis player; Dorothy Hamill, figure skater; Nadia Comaneci, gymnast; Kathy Kusner, jockey; Cindy Nelson, skier; and Judy Rankin, golfer.

Hanley, Reid M. WHO'S WHO IN TRACK AND FIELD. New Rochelle, N.Y.: Arlington House, 1973. 160 p.

Typical of most "Who's Who" books, this work provides only cursory biographical information for each of the athletes. Several women have been included, however, and the list ranges from well-known Babe Didrikson Zaharias of 1932 Olympic fame to record holders in the 1972 Olympic Games. Use of the book is hampered by lack of an index.

Hollander, Phyllis. AMERICAN WOMEN IN SPORTS. New York: Grossett and Dunlap, 1972. 112 p.

More than fifty brief sketches of American sportswomen in nine different activities have been compiled for this book. Selections range from such early champions as Eleanora Sears, Stella Walsh, Glenna Collett, and Gertrude Ederle to those of more recent years, Billie Jean King, Peggy Fleming, Kathy Whitworth, and Debbie Meyer. A separate chapter highlights the diverse career of Babe Didrikson Zaharias. Sports heroines from bowling, riding, tennis, swimming and diving, track and field, figure skating, golf, skiing, and channel swimming are included.

_____. 100 GREATEST WOMEN IN SPORTS. New York: Grosset and Dunlap, 1976. 142 p.

This book provides brief sketches of the exploits of more than one hundred women athletes in eighteen different sports and includes photographs of almost all of them. The text highlights the outstanding accomplishments of pioneers in the sports world in the early 1900s, such as Hazel Wightman and Eleanora Sears as well as modern champions such as Billie Jean King and Peggy Fleming, who now utilize their athletic talents as professionals. The author reviews women's successes as athletes since the turn of the century not only in sports which have long been the domain of the female --tennis, figure skating, and swimming--but also in areas only recently invaded by women--marathon running and horse racing.

Jacobs, Helen Hull. FAMOUS MODERN AMERICAN WOMEN ATHLETES. New York: Dodd, Mead and Co., 1975. 136 p.

The author provides brief biographies of eight American women who have achieved success in their different sports. Career highlights are included for Judy Cook Soutar, bowling; Janet Lynn, figure skating; Micki King, diving; Kathy Whitworth, golf; Cindy Nelson, skiing; Shirley Babashoff, swimming; Billie Jean King, tennis; and Francie Larrieu, track.

Jacobs, Karen Folger. GIRLSPORTS. New York: Bantam Books, 1978. 180 p. Paperbound.

Based on the author's personal interviews with fifteen young female athletes, this book describes their achievements in a variety of activities ranging from jacks to rodeo. Some, like Tai Babilonia, Olympic skater, are well known; others may never be known outside their own local community. Each, however, has been a successful competitor and knows what it is like to be the only girl on a boys' team; to work long grueling hours to become a champion; and to feel the real joy that comes from sports participation. In response to questions from the author, each of the young sportswomen talks about her interest in sports, her motivation to succeed, and her hopes for the future.

Jordan, Pat. BROKEN PATTERNS. New York: Dodd, Mead and Co., 1977. 213 p.

Several different sportswomen are portrayed in this book and are representative of some of the lesser known and less publicized activities in which women participate. Brief descriptions of the athletes and selected incidents in their sports careers are included for Willye White, track and field; Lillian Ellison, wrestler; Anne Henning, speed skating; Natalie Kahn, Cyndy Groffman, and Shirley Patterson, weight lifters; Shirley Muldowney, drag racer; and Joan Joyce and Donna Lapiano, softball. A more detailed account of the volleyball career of superstar winner, Mary Jo Peppler, is presented.

Lee, Mabel. MEMORIES OF A BLOOMER GIRL (1894-1924). Washington, D.C.: American Alliance for Health, Physical Education, and Recreation, 1977. 384 p.

Mabel Lee chronicles the first half of her professional career in
physical education, which spanned more than half a century.
While the book is based on the personal experiences of the author
and written in the form of memoirs, it does relate the role played
by one woman in advancing sports and physical education for women
in the United States at a time when the profession was new and
women who entered it were pioneers. Humorous anecdotes are
interspersed with the more serious aspects of the book which detail Lee's career from her early school days to 1924. It is the
story of one woman's involvement with sport, but is representative
of the lives of many women who entered the profession in its early
stages.

_____. MEMORIES BEYOND BLOOMERS (1924-1954). Washington, D.C.:
American Alliance for Health, Physical Education, and Recreation, 1978. 458 p.

This sequel to MEMORIES OF A BLOOMER GIRL continues the story
of Lee's professional career in physical education up to the time
of her retirement in 1954. She writes from first-hand experience
of her work in various professional organizations, her insights into
the organizational politics of such groups, and her tenure as the
first woman president of the American Physical Education Association. Of particular interest are her description of early developments in athletics for women and the continuing controversies sur-
rounding them. This second "memories" offers unusual insights into
the development of physical education for women and the early
days of women's athletics.

Leipold, L. Edmond. FAMOUS AMERICAN ATHLETES. Minneapolis: T.S.
Denison and Co., 1969. 83 p.

Two women have been included in this book, which presents biographies of ten athletes who rose to prominence in their selected
areas of endeavor. Brief career sketches are included for bowler
Shirley Rudolph Garms and figure skater Carol Heiss Jenkins. It
is difficult, however, to determine on what basis those selections
were made.

Macksey, Joan, and Macksey, Kenneth M. THE BOOK OF WOMEN'S
ACHIEVEMENTS. New York: Stein and Day, 1975. 288 p.

One of the chapters is devoted to sportswomen in this book which
reflects diverse accomplishments of women from artists to wartime
endeavors. Although the information is very brief with little biographical data, it does indicate the kinds of achievements women
have attained in sports. Fifty-five different women are mentioned
along with their major sporting accomplishments.

Martin, Ann. THE EQUESTRIAN WOMAN. New York: Grossett and Dunlap,
1979. 224 p.

Brief biographical sketches of twenty one equestriennes who participate in diverse activities from racing to driving are presented in this book. Emphasis is placed on riders in racing, hunting, and dressage events; thus, readers seeking information on persons in Western riding events such as barrel racing may find little of interest to them.

Robertson, Max, ed. THE ENCYCLOPEDIA OF TENNIS. New York: Viking Press, 1974. 392 p.

This book is encyclopedic in its coverage of tennis information, but does include several sections about women. Brief biographical data are provided for many well-known players ranging from Maud Watson, the first Wimbledon champion to Chris Evert and Evonne Goolagong of more recent fame. More detailed biographies for some women are found in a section titled "Great Players of All Time." "Centre Court Classics" describes five women's matches at Wimbledon considered to be among the best in tennis history, and "The Women's Pro Game" outlines the development of women's professional tennis. A section on fashion provides a colorful history of women's tennis costumes, and the records section lists the winners of major tennis tournaments. Many of the excellent photographs throughout the book are of women.

Ryan, Joan. CONTRIBUTIONS OF WOMEN: SPORTS. Minneapolis: Dillon Press, 1975. 136 p.

Biographies of six successful female athletes are featured in this book. Although necessarily brief, the biographies present career highlights for Babe Didrikson Zaharias, all-around sportswoman; Kathy Kusner, Olympic equestrienne; Wilma Rudolph, Olympic runner; Billie Jean King, tennis star; Peggy Fleming, champion figure skater; and Melissa Belote, young swimming champion. A final section is devoted to brief comments on the athletic careers of eight other women: Gertrude Ederle, Althea Gibson, Sonja Henie, Micki King, Helen Wills Moody, Cathy Rigby, Eleanora Sears, and Wyomia Tyus.

Sabin, Francene. WOMEN WHO WIN. New York: Random House, 1975. 171 p.

Brief biographies of fourteen women who have been champions in recent years are presented in this book. The author emphasizes the athletic achievements of women in the 1960s and 1970s who have helped prepare the way for others to attain success. Sketches are included for Billie Jean King; Janet Lynn; Cheryl Toussaint; Paula Sperber; Cathy Rigby; Micki King; Kathy Whitworth; the Cochran sisters, Marilyn, Barbara, and Lindy; and Jenny Bartz, Lynn Genesko, Nina MacInnis, and Sharon Berg, the first American women to receive nationally recognized swimming scholarships.

Scott, Eugene. TENNIS: A GAME OF MOTION. New York: Crown Publishers, 1973. 256 p.

Excellent photographs are the hallmark of this book, and perhaps half of the book is devoted to women. The chapter, "Different Strokes for Different Folks," is a gallery of action photographs with little narrative accompanying them. In "Aces," Scott provides a brief sketch and photograph of Helen Wills, Suzanne Lenglen, Maureen Connolly, Margaret Court, Evonne Goolagong, Chris Evert, and Billie Jean King. In a concluding chapter he details the historic matches of Lenglen and Wills in 1926, and Goolagong and Evert in 1971. Other sections also include photographs of women players; some are candid shots of unknown players, and others are of the best-known champions through the years.

Shane, George. SPORTRAITS OF THE STARS. Toronto: Gall Publications, 1975. 111 p. Paperbound.

A brief, one-page biography illustrated with a caricature drawing relates the achievement records of several men and women athletes. Women included are Janet Lynn, Shane Gould, Margaret Court, Annemarie Proell, Marlene Stewart Streit, Violetta Nesvkaitis, Olga Korbut, Karen Magnussen, Billie Jean King, and Sylvia Burka.

Stambler, Irwin. SPEED KINGS: WORLD'S FASTEST HUMANS. New York: Doubleday and Co., 1973. 162 p.

Two women are included in the author's selection of twelve of the "world's fastest humans." A brief biographical sketch of Chi Cheng, first Asian woman to win an Olympic medal, outlines her running career and describes in detail her record-breaking run of ten seconds in the 100-yard dash at a meet in Oregon in 1970. The section on swimmer Shane Gould, focuses entirely on her 1972 100-meter freestyle performance of 58.5 seconds, which made her the swimming world's fastest woman.

_____. WOMEN IN SPORTS. Garden City, N.Y.: Doubleday and Co., 1975. 155 p.

This book is introduced with a brief overview of the struggle women have had in achieving sports opportunities, and the remaining chapters review the individual accomplishments of sportswomen in several different fields of endeavor. Included are Cathy Rigby, gymnastics; Billie Jean King, tennis; Anne Henning, speed skating; Robyn Smith, horse racing; Wyomia Tyus, Mary Decker, and Babe Didrikson Zaharias, track and field; Melissa Belote, swimming; Shirley Muldowney, drag racing; Barbara Ann Cochran, skiing; Micki King, diving; and Theresa Shank, basketball.

Wise, S.F., and Fisher, Douglas. CANADA'S SPORTING HEROES. Don Mills, Ontario: General Publishing Co., 1974. 338 p.

Collections of Biographies

This book could be titled "Who's Who in Canadian Sport." Of the 174 biographical accounts of sports champions included, 28 are of women. All are sufficiently detailed to provide information about their careers and major sports accomplishments, and the selections range from champions in the early 1900s to the time of publication. All selections are members of Canada's Sports Hall of Fame.

Chapter 5

BIOGRAPHIES OF WOMEN IN SPECIFIC SPORTS

GOLF

Elliot, Len, and Kelly, Barbara. WHO'S WHO IN GOLF. New Rochelle, N.Y.: Arlington House Publishers, 1976. 208 p.

> Brief biographical data, including their major golf championships, are included for the top women golfers from as early as 1896. Criteria for selecting women players for the book, which also includes men, were (1) amateurs with two or more Curtis Cup team memberships or one World Cup membership, (2) professionals who had won at least once on the Ladies' PGA tour, and (3) All Americans who had won a national championship, amateur or professional.

Hahn, James, and Hahn, Lynn. NANCY LOPEZ: GOLFING PIONEER. St. Paul: EMC Corp., 1979. 40 p. Paperbound.

> This biography for young readers is the story of Nancy Lopez, the first Mexican American to achieve success on the Ladies Professional Golfer's Association (LPGA) tour. Lopez's early life and participation in golf are described, and the book concludes with her experiences after becoming a professional golfer in 1977.

Jacobs, Linda. LAURA BAUGH: GOLF'S GOLDEN GIRL. St. Paul: EMC Corp., 1975. 40 p. Paperbound.

> Written for young readers this brief biography sketches Laura Baugh's golf career from her first attempts with a handmade club at the age of four to her joining the professional ranks at eighteen. The author describes Baugh's early personal life and some of her interests other than golf.

O'Shea, Mary Jo. LAURA BAUGH. Mankato, Minn.: Creative Education, 1976. 31 p.

> This easy-to-read biography briefly details the golf career of Laura Baugh. Emphasis is placed on her early life and the experience that shaped her athletic success; the final pages describe her professional career, which began at the age of eighteen.

GYMNASTICS

Beecham, Justin. OLGA, HER LIFE AND HER GYMNASTICS. New York: Two Continents Publishing Groups, 1974. 128 p. Paperbound.

> While focusing on the life and gymnastic career of Olga Korbut, Beecham has also woven in an abbreviated history of the development of gymnastics and its place in the Olympic Games.

Burchard, S[ue].H. SPORTS STAR, NADIA COMANECI. New York: Harcourt Brace Jovanovich, 1977. 64 p.

> This brief biography of Rumanian gymnast Nadia Comaneci sketches the background that led to her outstanding performance in the 1976 Olympics. Her early life and training to become a gymnast and her "perfect score" performances at Montreal are described in an easy-to-read language for young children.

Grumeza, Ian. NADIA. New York: Hawthorn Books, 1977. 127 p. Paperbound.

> The life and brief career of champion gymnast Nadia Comaneci is chronicled in this book which describes the qualities that made her successful, the rigorous schedule that is part of being a champion, and some of the competitions in which she astounded audiences with her record-breaking performances.

Jacobs, Linda. CATHY RIGBY: ON THE BEAM. St. Paul: EMC Corp., 1975. 40 p. Paperbound.

> This brief biography for young readers sketches the life and career of gymnast Cathy Rigby, the first American to win a medal in international competition at the World Gymnastics Championships in Yugoslavia in 1970.

_____. JOAN MOORE RICE: THE OLYMPIC DREAM. St. Paul: EMC Corp., 1975. 40 p. Paperbound.

> This brief biography for young readers describes the gymnastic career of Olympic competitor, Joan Moore Rice, who gave up her dreams of participation in the 1976 Olympic Games to become a teacher of future Olympians. Her early introduction to gymnastics and her major successes in competition are described and generously illustrated with photographs.

_____. OLGA KORBUT, TEARS AND TRIUMPH. St. Paul: EMC Corp., 1974. 40 p. Paperbound.

> This biography for young readers sketches the highlights in the career of the Russian gymnast Olga Korbut. Her triumphs as a 1972 Olympic gold medalist and her subsequent drop to a second-place performer are described.

Krementz, Jill. A VERY YOUNG GYMNAST. New York: Alfred A. Knopf, 1978. 119 p.

> The narrative for this pictorial review of young gymnast Terrance York, is written in the first-person language of the ten-year-old performer. Events in the training and life of a gymnast are related, and the accompanying photographs by the author provide excellent illustrations of the activities of a "budding" gymnast.

McMillan, Constance V. NADIA COMANECI: ENCHANTED SPARROW. St. Paul: EMC Corporation, 1977. 40 p. Paperbound.

> The brief, but highly successful career of Rumanian gymnast, Nadia Comaneci, is described in this easy-to-read biography. The book outlines major events in her life from the time she was selected for coaching at the age of six to her outstanding achievement of seven perfect scores for performances in the 1976 Olympic Games. Many photographs appear throughout the book.

Miklowitz, Gloria D. NADIA COMANECI. New York: Grosset and Dunlap, 1977. 90 p. Paperbound.

> An easy-to-read biography for young people, this book highlights the events leading to the championship performance of Rumanian gymnast Nadia Comaneci in the 1976 Olympic Games.

Smith, Jay H. OLGA KORBUT. Mankato, Minn.: Creative Education, 1974. 31 p.

> This biography for children highlights the important events in the life and brief career of Russian gymnast Olga Korbut. The brevity of the book prevents any lengthy discussion of Korbut's achievements, but it does provide the reader with an overview of her life as a champion gymnast.

Sullivan, George. THE PICTURE STORY OF NADIA COMANECI. New York: Julian Messner, 1977. 64 p.

> Written for the young reader, this brief biography sketches the highlights in the short career of Rumanian Nadia Comaneci, the youngest gymnastics champion in the history of the Olympic Games and the first person to achieve a judge's perfect score of ten.

Suponev, Michael. OLGA KORBUT: A BIOGRAPHICAL PORTRAIT. Garden City, N.Y.: Doubleday and Co., 1975. 87 p.

> This biography of Soviet gymnast Olga Korbut stresses her career, the training and development of a champion, and the daily routine required to succeed as an Olympic star. Since the book is translated from Russian, it perhaps contains information not often included in biographies by other authors.

Taylor, Paula. GYMNASTICS' HAPPY SUPERSTAR, OLGA KORBUT. Mankato, Minn.: Creative Educational Society, 1977. 31 p.

> Written for young readers, each page of short narrative in this
> book has an accompanying photograph on the facing page. The
> book briefly sketches some of the difficult maneuvers Korbut per-
> forms and some of her major gymnastic accomplishments.

HORSEBACK RIDING AND RACING

Adler, Larry. YOUNG WOMEN IN THE WORLD OF RACE HORSES. New
York: David McKay Co., 1978. 56 p.

> Early chapters in this book describe the kinds of job possibilities
> available for women in the world of horse racing and the training
> and qualifications necessary for them. Brief sketches of several
> well-known women jockeys are included, and final sections discuss
> women harness racers and trainers and owners of thoroughbreds who
> are women.

Brown, Fern G. RACING AGAINST THE ODDS: ROBYN G. SMITH. Milwaukee: Raintree Editions, 1976. 47 p.

> In this brief biography for young readers, the author relates the
> events in Robyn Smith's struggle to become a jockey, even though
> she had never previously ridden a horse. Her experiences in learn-
> ing to ride, her first races, her later successes, and her continued
> effort to be accepted in the racing world are interestingly described
> by Brown.

Golden, Flora. WOMEN IN SPORTS: HORSEBACK RIDING. New York:
Harvey House, 1978. 70 p.

> A brief history of women's involvement in horseback riding intro-
> duces this book written for young readers. Types of riding competi-
> tion are explained, and biographical sketches of five women who
> have attained success in each of the different areas are included.
> The five are Denise Boudrot, jockey; Michele McEvoy, jumper;
> Hilda Gurney, dressage rider; Sue Sally Jones, polo player; and
> Helen Crabtree, show rider, coach, and trainer.

Haney, Lynn. THE LADY IS A JOCK. New York: Dodd, Mead and Co.,
1973. 180 p.

> Biographical sketches of four women jockeys are found in this book,
> which details the gypsy life of the female jockey. Often reverting
> to the vernacular of the turf, the author vividly describes the ca-
> reers of Barbara Jo Rubin, the first woman jockey who rose to
> fame and then slipped into obscurity after three accidents kept her
> from resuming her career; of Robyn Smith who left a potential act-
> ing career to follow the track; of Patty Barton who began her ca-

reer as a saddle bronc rider; and of the outspoken and often controversial Mary Bacon whose unusual antics both off and on the track frequently resulted in news sensationalism. Other chapters highlight some of the lesser-known women jockeys and comment briefly on several women who hold other posts as trainer, veterinarian, agent, groom, exercise girl, and valet in the racing profession. A final chapter explores the reasons women may choose professional careers in racing and some of the psychological aspects of women's interest in horses.

Jacobs, Linda. ROBYN SMITH: IN SILKS. St. Paul: EMC Corp., 1976. 40 p. Paperbound.

The story of Robyn Smith's efforts to become a jockey, even though she had never been on a horse, makes interesting reading for young readers. The author relates Smith's early experiences in the racing world after giving up the idea of an acting career, and finally her experiences in New York as a reasonably successful jockey, one of the very few women in the profession.

Krementz, Jill. A VERY YOUNG RIDER. New York: Alfred A. Knopf, 1978. 119 p.

This book is written as if ten-year-old Vivi Malloy is relating her own ideas about horses and riding. Responsibilities in caring for and owning a horse are described, as well as the hard work and dedication necessary to become a competitive rider. Krementz's photographs provide as much information as the narrative. Young horse lovers will find the book especially appealing.

McGinnis, Vera. RODEO ROAD: MY LIFE AS A PIONEER COWGIRL. New York: Hastings House, 1974. 225 p.

This autobiography by McGinnis, one of the pioneers of women's rodeo, chronicles her riding career from the time of her first stunt at the age of three, leaping an irrigation ditch on a burro, to the abrupt conclusion of her rodeo riding in 1934 at thirty-nine, as a result of a serious fall from her horse which left her near death. Her colorful descriptions of the world of rodeo are sprinkled with personal anecdotes that occurred as she traveled the circuit that included the usual rodeos held in the United States, as well as exhibition riding in the Orient and the British Isles. The book is generously illustrated with photographs; those, with the text, provide a general history of women in the rodeo.

Van Steenwyk, Elizabeth. WOMEN IN SPORTS: RODEO. New York: Harvey House, 1978. 78 p.

A brief history of the development of rodeo for women introduces this book and is followed by a description of the seven standard events in which women participate. Sketches of the rodeo activities of several young women competitors are provided along with a brief review of the antics of professional rodeo clown Benjie Prudom.

MOTORCYCLING AND AUTO RACING

Butcher, Grace. WOMEN IN SPORTS: MOTORCYCLING. New York: Harvey House, 1976. 63 p.

This volume is devoted primarily to competitive motorcycle racing and describes the different types of racing events. The author gives a brief introduction to the special equipment used and the techniques of learning to ride. Some of the exploits of eight women racers are presented in "capsule" sketches of their entry into and involvement with motorcycling.

Dolan, Edward F., Jr., and Lyttle, Richard B. JANET GUTHRIE, FIRST WOMAN DRIVER AT INDIANAPOLIS. Garden City, N.Y.: Doubleday and Co., 1978. 80 p.

In this short biography of the first woman to break the male barrier and race at the Indianapolis 500, the authors describe her early life, her interest in flying, followed by her interest in auto racing, which culminated in her qualifying for the best-known race in the United States.

Hahn, James, and Hahn, Lynn. JANET GUTHRIE: CHAMPION RACER. St. Paul: EMC Corp., 1979. 40 p. Paperbound.

This biography for young readers focuses on the career of Janet Guthrie, the first woman driver to qualify for the annual Indianapolis 500 mile auto race. Guthrie's early life is described briefly as well as the struggles she faced in attempting to break into the masculine domain of auto racing. The book is liberally illustrated with photographs of Guthrie.

MOUNTAINEERING

Morin, Nea. A WOMAN'S REACH, MOUNTAINEERING MEMOIRS. New York: Dodd, Mead and Co., 1968. 288 p.

The challenge of the mountains is vividly described in this personal account of Morin's long and remarkable climbing career. She writes descriptively of the major climbs she attempted from 1922 to 1959 when her serious climbing endeavors were curtailed because of osteoarthritis in the hip joint. The elation and exhilaration voiced by climbers is evident in the author's record of her long involvement with climbing.

Underhill, Miriam. GIVE ME THE HILLS. Riverside, Conn.: Chatham Press, 1971. 278 p.

This book is a personal account of the author's "love affair" with the mountains. She describes in detail her mountaineering exploits that spanned over forty years and ranged over peaks in both Europe and the United States. Her pioneering efforts in "manless" climbing with no male guides are described as well as winter climbs of the New Hampshire "four thousand footers." Numerous photographs appear throughout the book contributing to the feeling of joyful adventure that pervades the text.

Williams, Cicely. WOMEN ON THE ROPE. London: George Allen and Unwin, 1973. 240 p.

In a chronological account of the activities of women mountaineers, Williams writes a descriptive history of women's participation in mountain climbing. Her colorful accounts of nineteenth-century women, the "petticoat pioneers" who climbed in long dresses and crinoline petticoats, are followed by the feats of seasoned climbers of the twentieth century, such as Yvette Vaucher, first woman included in a Mt. Everest expedition. The book should be of special interest to mountain climbing enthusiasts.

SKIING AND ICE SKATING

Burchard, S[ue].H. SPORTS STAR, DOROTHY HAMILL. New York: Harcourt Brace Jovanovich, 1978. 63 p.

This large-print book for very young readers highlights the brief skating career of Dorothy Hamill from receipt of her first skates at the age of eight to her winning the Olympic Gold Medal in 1976. Her performances in winning the United States championship in 1974 and the World Championship in 1976 are described, as well as the training and discipline necessary for becoming a champion.

Jacobs, Linda. ANNEMARIE PROELL: QUEEN OF THE MOUNTAIN. St. Paul: EMC Corp., 1975. 40 p. Paperbound.

This biography for young readers sketches the career of Annemarie Proell, the Austrian skier who had won thirty-one individual races, a record unmatched by any other skier, male or female. Much of the book focuses on Proell's attitude toward winning and losing and the ways in which she handles that aspect of competition.

_____. CINDY NELSON: NORTH COUNTRY SKIER. St. Paul: EMC Corp., 1976. 40 p. Paperbound.

This book for young readers is a brief biographical sketch of Cindy Nelson, downhill skier, who won the World Cup title at Grindewald, Switzerland, after recovering from a serious injury suffered in the same place two years before. The author describes her early life in Lutsen, Minnesota, where she learned to ski and developed into a champion at her parents' ski resort.

———. JANET LYNN: SUNSHINE ON ICE. St. Paul: EMC Corp., 1974. 40 p. Paperbound.

This brief biography for young readers captures the "sunshine" personality of figure skater Janet Lynn. The author describes her introduction to skates at the age of two and a half and follows her career to her joining the professional ranks at the age of twenty. The book also emphasizes the importance of Lynn's strong religious beliefs in her personal and professional life.

May, Julian. JANET LYNN: FIGURE SKATING STAR. Mankato, Minn.: Crestwood House, 1975. 48 p.

This brief biography for young readers sketches the highlights of Janet Lynn's amateur career. Her introduction to skating and early successes are described, as well as her failure to win the coveted gold medal in either the Olympic Games in 1972 or the World Championships in 1973.

Morse, Ann. JANET LYNN. Mankato, Minn.: Creative Educational Society, 1975. 31 p.

Written for very young readers this book briefly describes the high points of Janet Lynn's successful skating career in 1973. The successes and the failures of the young woman who won several skating medals yet seemed to lack the strong desire to win, are described in simple, readable terms.

Morse, Charles, and Morse, Ann. PEGGY FLEMING. Mankato, Minn.: Creative Education, 1974. 31 p.

Written for young readers, this brief biography sketches the major events in Peggy Fleming's figure skating career leading to her gold-medal performance in the 1968 Olympics.

Schmitz, Dorothy C. DOROTHY HAMILL, SKATE TO VICTORY. Mankato, Minn.: Crestwood House, 1977. 47 p.

In language for young readers Schmitz details the rise to stardom of figure skater, Dorothy Hamill. The dedication and desire necessary to become a champion are related in the biography which begins with Hamill's first skating efforts at the age of eight to her Olympic success in 1976 and subsequent entry into professional skating with the Ice Capades. The book is generously illustrated with photographs.

Smith, Jay H. ROSI MITTERMAIER. Mankato, Minn.: Creative Educational Society, 1977. 31 p.

This brief sketch of German skier Rosi Mittermaier, written for young readers, focuses primarily on her performance at the 1976 Winter Olympic Games. The author describes her experiences in winning three medals at the games at the age of twenty-five when most women skiers have retired from major competition.

Smith, Miranda G. DOROTHY HAMILL. Mankato, Minn.: Creative Educational Society, 1977. 31 p.

This brief biography for young readers focuses primarily on the 1976 Olympics and Dorothy Hamill's gold-medal performance there. A brief description of her training to become a champion in spite of her lack of self-confidence is also provided.

Soucheray, Joe. SHEILA YOUNG. Mankato, Minn.: Creative Educational Society, 1977. 31 p.

This book is a brief biography for young readers of the first American to win three medals in the Winter Olympics. Highlights of Sheila Young's championship speedskating, in which she won the medals at Innsbruck, and bicycling, in which she has also been a champion, are described in easily readable language.

Van Steenwyk, Elizabeth. PEGGY FLEMING: CAMEO OF A CHAMPION. New York: McGraw-Hill Book Co., 1978. 132 p.

This biography of Peggy Fleming is essentially the story of her career as an amateur figure skater. Van Steenwyk begins with her transition from violin lessons to skating lessons as a nine year old and progresses through the various experiences in her rise to champion status. The major competitions in which she participated are described, concluding with her gold-medal victory in the 1968 Olympics. A brief epilogue outlines her life after the Olympic victory.

_____. WOMEN IN SPORTS: FIGURE SKATING. New York: Harvey House, 1976. 79 p.

This small volume, one in a series that focuses on a variety of sports in which women participate, presents brief biographical sketches of five champion North American skaters: Peggy Fleming, Janet Lynn, Karen Magnussen, Dianne deLeeuw, and Dorothy Hamill. The book is introduced with a short review of the historical development of figure skating and includes the basic rules and elements of competition for the sport.

Walter, Claire. WOMEN IN SPORTS: SKIING. New York: Harvey House, 1977. 63 p.

Brief highlights in the ski racing careers of Barbara Ann Cochran, Annemarie Moser-Proell, and Cindy Nelson are presented in this book along with cross-country racing competitor, Jana Hlavaty. A separate section describes the fairly new competitive event, free-style or "hot dog" skiing, and notes the accomplishments of Suzy

Chaffee, Judy Nagel, Genia Fuller, and others in this professional skiing event.

SWIMMING, SCUBA DIVING, AND SAILING

Francis, Clare. COME HELL OR HIGH WATER. London: Pelham Books, 1977. 198 p.

This book is a personal account of the author's participation in the 1976 Singlehanded Transatlantic Race from Plymouth, England, to Newport, Rhode Island. She details the problems of sailing in heavy seas, fog, and among icebergs to finish in thirteenth place in twenty-nine days. The book provides insight into why sailors are willing to risk their lives on long ocean voyages in spite of the loneliness and rigors that must be endured.

_____. WOMAN ALONE. New York: David McKay Co., 1977. 184 p.

This book is almost identical to the author's other book, COME HELL OR HIGH WATER. Only minor changes such as the addition of a word or phrase in a few places are evident, and some of the photographs used for illustration are different. Otherwise, the two books are identical.

Gleasner, Diana C. WOMEN IN SPORTS: SWIMMING. New York: Harvey House, 1975. 63 p.

A cursory review of the history of swimming introduces this volume and is followed by brief highlights in the aquatic careers of diver Christine Loock; speed swimmers Shirley Babashoff and Kathy Heddy; synchronized swimmer Gail Buzonas; and marathon swimmer Diana Nyad.

Hass, Lotte. GIRL ON THE OCEAN FLOOR. London: George C. Harrap and Co., 1972. 166 p.

Hass vividly describes her experiences as the only woman to accompany a 1949 expedition to make the first dives in the shark-infested Red Sea for the purpose of making an underwater film. Although Lotte Beierl begins as a secretary to Hans Hass, well-known underwater diver, and is finally allowed to go on the expedition primarily to keep records and do the "housekeeping chores," she soon proves herself as an accomplished diver and photographer. She provides descriptive accounts of the many unusual events that occurred on the expedition, which culminated in a prize-winning film and the marriage of Lotte and Hans.

Hauser, Hillary. WOMEN IN SPORTS: SCUBA DIVING. New York: Harvey House, 1976. 79 p.

Brief sketches of highlights in the lives of five women involved in underwater careers are included in this volume. Each of the five, Valerie Taylor, Eugenie Clark, Kati Garner, Zale Parry, and Sylvia Earle, is representative of the diverse occupations available to women in diving from U.S. Navy diver to underwater actress.

Jacobs, Linda. SHANE GOULD: OLYMPIC SWIMMER. St. Paul: EMC Corp., 1974. 40 p. Paperbound.

Written for young readers, this brief biography of Australian swimmer Shane Gould outlines the rigorous training and personal sacrifice which led to her winning five medals in the 1972 Olympics at the age of fifteen. The author describes Gould's early family life and provides some insight into the joys and the difficulties of being in the public spotlight at such a young age.

Libman, Gary. LYNNE COX. Mankato, Minn.: Creative Educational Society, 1977. 31 p.

This easy-to-read book sketches the accomplishments of teenage channel swimmer Lynne Cox. Brief accounts of her championship swims in channels all over the world are interspersed with some of her own thoughts about long-distance swimming.

Nyad, Diana. OTHER SHORES. New York: Random House, 1978. 174 p.

Author Nyad provides a personal account of her record-setting achievements as a marathon swimming champion. She explains the in-depth training required for the accomplishments she has attained, as well as the sensory deprivation and almost hypnotic sensation that occurs in such long-distance swims. She concludes the book with details of preparation for her highly publicized swim from Havana, Cuba, to Marathon, Florida.

TENNIS

Baker, Jim. BILLIE JEAN KING. New York: Grosset and Dunlap Publishers, 1974. 90 p. Paperbound.

Although this book written for young sports fans describes King's early life and amateur career, the major portion is devoted to her activities in professional tennis, including her work as player-coach with World Team Tennis. Her views on women's rights and her efforts to gain equity for women in tennis are described. A chronological list of all of King's major championships through 1974 concludes the volume.

Burchard, Marshall, and Burchard, Sue [H.]. SPORTS HERO, BILLIE JEAN KING. New York: G.P. Putnam's Sons, 1975. 95 p.

Written in very simple terms for the second- to fifth-grade reader, this large-print book relates the story of Billie Jean King's tennis career. Chapters are devoted to King's learning to play the game on the public courts of Long Beach, her decision to make tennis her career, her first Wimbledon championship, her rise to number-one ranking, her move to professional player, and her much publicized match with Bobby Riggs. A concluding chapter describes some of her activities as she attempts to upgrade the sport of tennis for women, particularly in the professional realm.

Burchard, Sue [H.]. CHRIS EVERT. New York: Harcourt Brace Jovanovich, 1976. 64 p.

Written in large print for the young reader, this book briefly highlights the tennis career of Chris Evert, including her amateur successes and her professional tennis endeavors. Brief glimpses into her personal life are also provided.

Court, Margaret Smith, and McGann, George. COURT ON COURT: A LIFE OF TENNIS. New York: Dodd, Mead and Co., 1975. 211 p.

In this autobiography Court outlines her introduction to tennis as a young child in Albury, Australia, her early touring and success as an amateur, and her induction into professional tennis. She writes about her concern for the demise of good sportsmanship and the loss of the amateur spirit in tennis as money becomes an increasingly important factor in the professional circuit. She is candid in her admiration for the skill of many of her competitors, but critical of players when she believes "big money" has made a change in attitude and relationships with others.

Davidson, Owen, and Jones, C.M. GREAT WOMEN TENNIS PLAYERS. London: Pelham Books, 1971. 142 p.

This book presents brief sketches of the tennis playing careers of women champions ranging from "early greats," Charlotte Cooper, Charlotte Dod (who became the youngest Wimbledon champion in history when she won the singles in 1887 at fifteen), and seven-time Wimbledon champion, Dorothea Douglas Chambers, to Maria Bueno, Margaret Court, and Billie Jean King. Included also, are "isolated immortals," Cilli Aussem, Lili d'Alvarez, Molla Mallory, and Dorothy Round. Information is focused on the tennis feats of the individual players with particular reference to their wins at Wimbledon.

Dolan, Edward F., Jr., and Lyttle, Richard B. MARTINA NAVRATILOVA. Garden City, N.Y.: Doubleday and Co., 1977. 81 p.

Young sports fans should find interesting reading in this biography of the Czechoslovakian tennis player who defected to the United States in order to have freedom to pursue her tennis career. The authors have outlined her early life and tennis pursuits and have captured the dynamic personality that has made her a favorite among American fans. Her major amateur successes are described, as well as the highlights of her play as a professional.

Gemme, Leila Boyle. KING ON THE COURT: BILLIE JEAN KING. Milwaukee: Raintree Editions, 1976. 47 p.

This book for young readers describes King's introduction to and progress in amateur tennis and her major championship successes. The latter half of the book relates her efforts to change tennis from a sport for the wealthy only, to one for the "average guy" and her often criticized work as a professional player attempting to gain equity for women in the sport.

Gibson, Althea, with Curtis, Richard. SO MUCH TO LIVE FOR. New York: G.P. Putnam's Sons, 1968. 160 p.

Gibson has written only a partial story of her life covering the years from 1958 to 1968. Biographical data are covered in the introduction by Curtis, but the author begins with her retirement from amateur tennis in 1958 after distinguishing herself as the first Negro woman to win British and American championships. Succeeding chapters are devoted to her efforts at a singing career, her brief stint in a movie, her tour as a lecturer for a bread company, and the disastrous financial results of trying to manage her own tennis exhibition tour. The beginning of her golf career at the age of thirty-three concludes this autobiography of one segment of Gibson's versatile career.

Glickman, William G. WINNERS ON THE TENNIS COURT. New York: Franklin Watts, 1978. 48 p.

In this book for juveniles, three of the most recent women tennis champions are included. Highlights in the careers of Evonne Goolagong and Chris Evert are covered. Billie Jean King, perhaps the best known of the three, warrants only four short paragraphs because entire books have been written about her, and the author felt her career was more than adequately covered in those.

Goolagong, Evonne, and Collins, Bud. EVONNE! ON THE MOVE. New York: E.P. Dutton and Co., 1975. 190 p.

Goolagong's autobiography is neither a chronological detailing of her life nor an in-depth review of her brief career as a tennis competitor. Rather, it is a personal account of her introduction to the sport, her rise to the top, and, ultimately, her move into the professional tennis world. The book is sprinkled with anecdotes about life with her family, her coach and mentor, Vic Edwards, and traveling on the tennis circuit. It provides an overview of one woman's rise to tennis fame, in this case, an unusual accomplishment considering her background as an aborigine, "the brown-skinned descendant of wandering boomerang throwers" from the Australian outback.

Hahn, James, and Hahn, Lynn. TRACY AUSTIN: POWERHOUSE IN PINA-FORE. St. Paul: EMC Corp., 1978. 40 p.

This brief biography of Tracy Austin, youngest tennis player ever to compete in the prestigious Wimbledon tournament, sketches her life and short tennis career in language for young readers.

Haney, Lynn. CHRIS EVERT, THE YOUNG CHAMPION. New York: G.P. Putnam's Sons, 1976. 127 p.

This biography of Chris Evert focuses primarily on her professional tennis career although brief sections describe her early years in tennis and her amateur successes. In describing Evert's major professional experiences Haney has also woven in information about several of her competitors. Julie Anthony, Evonne Goolagong, Martina Navratilova, and Billie Jean King all receive more than cursory mention by the author, and more photographs of other well-known women players appear than of Evert.

Herda, D.J. FREE SPIRIT: EVONNE GOOLAGONG. Milwaukee: Raintree Editions, 1976. 47 p.

Written for young readers, this biography of Evonne Goolagong from the Australian outback, traces her rise from "ball girl" at the age of five to Wimbledon champion at nineteen. Her major championships are described, and her activities after joining the professional circuit complete the story of the young aboriginal tennis player who is expected to be a millionaire by the age of thirty.

Higdon, Hal. CHAMPIONS OF THE TENNIS COURT. Englewood Cliffs, N.J.: Prentice-Hall, 1971. 60 p.

Very brief biographical sketches of four women champions are included in this collection of eleven minibiographies. Highlights in the careers of Suzanne Lenglen, Helen Wills, Maureen Connolly, and Billie Jean King are presented in a two- to three-page narrative for each of them.

Jacobs, Helen Hull. GALLERY OF CHAMPIONS. Freeport, N.Y.: Books for Libraries Press, 1949. 1970. 224 p.

This book is a collection of personal remembrances by Jacobs of fifteen players against whom she competed during her tennis career. The selections have been ranked by the author in the order of importance according to her evaluation. Beginning with Suzanne Lenglen, minibiographies are included for Helen Wills Roark,

Hilde Krahvinkle Sperling, Alice Marble, Dorothy Round Little, Molla Bjurstedt Mallory, Pauline Betz, Simone Mathieu, Cilli Aussem, Sarah Polfrey Cooke, Anita Lizona Ellis, Louise Brough, Margaret Osborne duPont, Betty Nuthall, and Margaret Scriven Vivien.

Jacobs, Linda. CHRIS EVERT: TENNIS PRO. St. Paul: EMC Corp., 1974. 40 p. Paperbound.

In this biography for young readers, Jacobs provides an overview of the life and career of tennis player Chris Evert. The author emphasizes Evert's determination to "be herself" and the personal characteristics which have given her the name, "Little Miss Cool." Much of the book focuses on her career after becoming a professional player at the age of eighteen.

_____. EVONNE GOOLAGONG: SMILES AND SMASHES. St. Paul: EMC Corp., 1975. 40 p. Paperbound.

This book for young readers begins with Goolagong's 1971 Wimbledon championship then goes back to the beginning of her tennis career in Barellan, Australia. The influence of her coach, Victor Edwards, in her rise to successful amateur and professional play is described. The book also offers some insight into Goolagong's personal feelings about herself as a well-known tennis personality.

_____. MARTINA NAVRATILOVA: TENNIS FURY. St. Paul: EMC Corp., 1976. 40 p. Paperbound.

In language for young readers, Jacobs describes the growing-up years of Navratilova in Czechoslovakia and the efforts of her parents to steer her into a "sport for girls." Her successes as a tennis champion are covered, as well as the problems with government control of her career and her decision to seek asylum in the United States in 1975. The book also captures a feeling for the vibrant personality of Navratilova.

_____. ROSEMARY CASALS: THE REBEL ROSEBUD. St. Paul: EMC Corp., 1975. 40 p. Paperbound.

Written for youth, this book briefly outlines Rosie Casal's tennis career, focusing primarily on her experiences as a professional player. Her beginning interest in tennis is described along with some of the incidents that contributed to her being called a "rebel" among the tennis set.

Jones, Ann. A GAME TO LOVE. London: Stanley Paul and Co., 1971. 180 p.

This autobiography of 1969 Wimbledon champion, Ann Jones (nee Haydon), begins with her early life and progresses through her successful tennis career. Jones writes freely of her successes and failures, and her brief career as a table tennis competitor provides an added dimension to her story. The details of her participation in many different competitions offer interesting insight into the world of tennis.

King, Billie Jean, with Chapin, Kim. BILLIE JEAN. London: W.H. Allen, 1975. 208 p.

This detailed autobiography is a thorough analysis of Billie Jean King's tennis career. She writes at length about her growing up years in Long Beach, her budding interest in tennis, and her successes and failures as an amateur. A good portion of the book is devoted to her career in professional tennis and particularly her crusade for equity for women players. She writes candidly about her abortion and the unpleasant publicity associated with it. Her highly publicized match with Bobby Riggs is described in detail.

May, Julian. BILLIE JEAN KING: TENNIS CHAMPION. Mankato, Minn.: Crestwood House, 1974. 48 p.

King's displeasure with the stringent regulations in amateur tennis regularly creeps into the narrative of this brief biography for young readers. The book begins with her childhood introduction to tennis, progresses chronologically through her career, and concludes with the famous King-Riggs match in 1973. Major biographical data for King are provided in a separate section.

_____. CHRIS EVERT: PRINCESS OF TENNIS. Mankato, Minn.: Crestwood House, 1975. 48 p.

This brief narrative of the tennis career of Chris Evert is generously illustrated with photographs of the champion in action. Written in easy-to-read language the book depicts the highlights of Evert's tennis playing from her first lessons to her participation in professional tennis.

_____. FOREST HILLS AND THE AMERICAN TENNIS CHAMPIONSHIP. Mankato, Minn.: Creative Educational Society, 1976. 47 p.

Written for young readers, this book sketches the highlights in the tennis careers of several Forest Hills champions, both men and women. Molla Bjurstedt Mallory, Suzanne Lenglen, Helen Wills, and Helen Hull Jacobs are included in one section. Separate discussions are devoted to Alice Marble, Maureen Connolly, Althea Gibson, Billie Jean King, and Chris Evert. A list of men and women champions at Forest Hills through 1975 concludes the book.

_____. WIMBLEDON WORLD TENNIS FOCUS. Mankato, Minn.: Creative Education, 1975. 47 p.

This brief history of the world champion tennis tournament at Wimbledon is written for young readers and includes brief sketches of several women singles champions. May Sutton, Suzanne Lenglen, Helen Wills, Louise Brough, Helen Hull Jacobs, Maureen Connolly, and Althea Gibson are mentioned; Gussie Moran, Margaret Court, Evonne Goolagong, Billie Jean King, and Chris Evert are treated in more detail. A complete list of Wimbledon Singles champions for both women and men through 1974 is included.

Meade, Marion. WOMEN IN SPORTS: TENNIS. New York: Harvey House, 1975. 78 p.

The author describes major events in the rise to stardom of top-ranked players Billie Jean King, Rosemary Casals, Chris Evert, Evonne Goolagong Cawley, and Margaret Court. Meade also notes the problems encountered by women in attempting to achieve the financial success now possible in professional tennis.

Miklowitz, Gloria D. TRACY AUSTIN. New York: Grossett and Dunlap, 1978. 87 p. Paperbound.

In this easy-to-read book the author details the very brief career of young tennis star, Tracy Austin, the youngest player ever to compete at Wimbledon. The tennis successes of the entire Austin family (parents, Tracy's older sister, and three older brothers) are described briefly, but the major focus of the book is on Tracy's very quick rise to championship status. The book is generously illustrated with photographs of Tracy in action.

Morse, Ann. TENNIS CHAMPION, BILLIE JEAN KING. Mankato, Minn.: Creative Education Society, 1976. 31 p.

This brief book for very young readers is more a description of King, the person, than a chronicle of her tennis successes. Discussion of her major championships are not included, though the King-Riggs match is mentioned. Each short page of narrative has an accompanying photograph on the facing page.

Morse, Charles, and Morse, Ann. EVONNE GOOLAGONG. Mankato, Minn.: Amecus Street, 1974. 31 p.

This brief biography for young readers focuses on the early life of tennis champion Evonne Goolagong, and describes the major events leading to her championship at Wimbledon in 1971.

Olsen, James T. BILLIE JEAN KING: THE LADY OF THE COURT. Mankato, Minn.: Creative Education, 1974. 31 p.

This book describes King's tennis career as a successful amateur and her work in trying to change the sport, particularly for women. Written for young readers, the book highlights not only her major tennis championships, but some of the important incidents in her personal life as well.

O'Shea, Mary Jo. WINNING TENNIS STAR: CHRIS EVERT. Mankato, Minn.: Creative Educational Society, 1977. 31 p.

Action photos accompany each page of this brief biographical sketch of Chris Evert written for children. Information is focused primarily on her life and personality rather than on the major competitions in her tennis career.

Phillips, Betty Lou. CHRIS EVERT, FIRST LADY OF TENNIS. New York: Julian Messner, 1977. 189 p.

This biography of Chris Evert chronicles her rise to tennis fame from the earliest lessons with her father at the age of six to her attainment of the title, "world's top-ranked woman tennis player." Her early triumphs as a young amateur, her move into the professional world, and her success as a money-making tennis player are interspersed with brief glimpses into her personal life.

Robison, Nancy. TRACY AUSTIN, TEENAGE SUPERSTAR. New York: Harvey House Publishers, 1978. 63 p.

This book is a detailed biography for young readers of the brief life and career of tennis player Tracy Austin. The book opens with an account of Austin's performance at Wimbledon in 1977 when she advanced to the final match at the age of fourteen. Details of her early interest in tennis and her major accomplishments as an amateur in the sport follow.

Sabin, Francene. SET POINT, THE STORY OF CHRIS EVERT. New York: G.P. Putnam's Sons, 1977. 127 p.

Sabin's biography of tennis champion Chris Evert focuses particularly on the warm, family relationship in the Evert household and the continuing support provided by her parents. Early chapters describe Evert's introduction to tennis and her achievements as a young champion. Concluding chapters are devoted to her successful rise as an adult competitor and her move into the professional ranks at the age of eighteen. Brief attention is given to Evert's personal life, especially her aborted engagement to Jimmy Connors, but the book is primarily concerned with her major tennis accomplishments.

Smith, Jay H. CHRIS EVERT. Mankato, Minn.: Creative Education Society, 1975. 31 p.

This biography for young readers presents brief highlights in the tennis career of Chris Evert, including her first Wimbledon championship in 1974.

Sullivan, George. QUEENS OF THE COURT. New York: Dodd, Mead and Co., 1974. 111 p.

The author provides résumés of the careers of six well-known tennis professionals, Margaret Court, Rosemary Casals, Billie Jean King, Chris Evert, Evonne Goolagong, and Virginia Wade. In a concluding section, Sullivan briefly comments on the important contributions to the development of tennis made by leading women players in the early growing years of the sport.

Thacher, Alida M. RAISING A RACKET: ROSEMARY CASALS. Milwaukee: Raintree Editions, 1976. 47 p.

The tennis career of Rosie Casals, who regularly defied convention in her rise to championship status, is outlined in this book for young readers. The major portion of the book deals with her move to professional tennis and her attempts to improve the opportunities for women in that area.

Wade, Virginia, with Wallace, Mary Lou. COURTING TRIUMPH. New York: Mayflower Books, 1978. 192 p.

Wade provides a detailed account of her 1977 win at Wimbledon, interspersed with interesting tales of her personal life and her rise to tennis success. She provides an animated description of what she calls her "two tennis lives"--an instinctive, spontaneous kind of play followed by a more mature, intellectual, and professional approach to the game. She writes candidly of her problem with self-direction and developing the strong "will to win" so necessary for achieving success. Wade's description of her championship match at Wimbledon in 1977, after sixteen years of playing in that tournament, provides a provocative study of the thoughts and feelings of a top-flight player under the pressure of the final match on center court. Tennis enthusiasts, especially, should enjoy Wade's story.

TRACK AND FIELD

Connolly, Olga. THE RINGS OF DESTINY. New York: David McKay Co., 1968. 311 p.

This book is the personal story of the "Olympic romance" between Czechoslovakian discus thrower, Olga Fikotova, and United States hammer thrower, Harold Connolly, which culminated in their marriage only after special permission from the Czechoslovakian government.

Emery, David (retold by Kenneth, John). LILLIAN. London: Blackie and Son, 1973. 90 p.

Highlights in the brief career of British runner Lillian Board are described in this biography. The author relates her major wins in international competition, including a silver medal in the Mexico City Olympic Games when she missed the gold in the 400-meter run by one-tenth of a second. The final chapters detail her losing battle to cancer, which cut short a promising career and took her life at the age of twenty-two.

Gleasner, Diana C. WOMEN IN SPORTS: TRACK AND FIELD. New York: Harvey House Publishers, 1977. 77 p.

This book is introduced with a brief historical review of track and field for women. The remaining chapters are brief biographical sketches of runners Thelma Wright and Robin Campbell; hurdler Patty van Wolvelaere; high jumper Joni Huntley; javelin thrower Kathy Schmidt; and pentathlete Jane Frederick.

Huey, Lynda. A RUNNING START. New York: Quadrangle/New York Times Book Co., 1976. 241 p.

The world of the female athlete, with all the pleasures it offers and all the struggles necessary to achieve success in it, is portrayed in this often frank, descriptive book written by a woman runner and based on seventeen years of personal diaries. The author vividly details her experiences as a track athlete and her involvement with some of the more dramatic sports events in recent years--her relationships with athletes at San Jose State who were later involved in the Olympic Boycott Movement in 1968; teaching at Oberlin College in the controversial program instigated by Jack Scott; and her participation with Wilt's Wonder Women, a LaJolla track club sponsored by Wilt Chamberlain. Throughout the book she emphasizes the real joy found in sports participation, the problems women face in becoming successful athletes, and the strong pressures on women to conform to the female norm--submissive, nurturing, unathletic.

Jackson, Madeline Manning (as told to Jenkins, Jerry B.). RUNNING FOR JESUS. Waco, Tex.: Word, 1977. 192 p.

In this autobiography Olympic gold medalist, Madeline Jackson, describes her early childhood years and the beginning of her athletic career as a runner. She details the major successes she has achieved as a runner, as well as the problems she faced in attaining those goals. Jackson stresses the importance of her devout religion in her personal life and in her athletic career.

Jacobs, Linda. MADELINE MANNING JACKSON: RUNNING ON FAITH. St. Paul: EMC Corp., 1976. 39 p. Paperbound.

In easy-to-read language the author provides a brief account of highlights in the life of runner Madeline Jackson, who won a gold medal in the 1968 Olympics and then a silver in the 1972 Olympics after the birth of her first child. The book also emphasizes Jackson's religious devotion and its effect on her life.

_____. MARY DECKER: SPEED RECORDS AND SPAGHETTI. St. Paul: EMC Corp., 1975. 40 p. Paperbound.

This biography for young readers relates the highlights in the brief track career of Mary Decker, the fifteen-year-old who has already broken world speed records. Glimpses of her personal life are presented along with anecdotes of some of the unusual occurrences in her competitions.

_____. ROBIN CAMPBELL: JOY IN THE MORNING. St. Paul: EMC Corp., 1976. 40 p. Paperbound.

This biography for young readers is devoted primarily to the personal life of Robin Campbell, her introduction to running at the age of nine, and her growing successes, which make her a possible contender in the 1980 Olympic Games.

_____. WILMA RUDOLPH: RUN FOR GLORY. St. Paul: EMC Corp., 1975. 40 p. Paperbound.

Written for young readers this biography sketches the life and running career of Wilma Rudolph, first woman to win three gold medals in track in a single Olympics. Her early struggle with polio, which threatened to leave her a lifetime invalid, is followed by her career at Tennessee State, where she had been given a track scholarship. The book concludes with a brief section on her life as a wife, a mother, and a career woman.

Johnson, William O., and Williamson, Nancy. WHATTA GAL! THE BABE DIDRIKSON STORY. Boston: Little, Brown, 1977. 224 p.

This book chronicles the "Babe's" rise to athletic stardom and highlights the outstanding sports conquests that led many to declare her to be the greatest woman athlete in history. Much of the information has been gathered from personal interviews with individuals who knew her intimately: her older sister Lillie; physical education teacher Bea Lytle; Olympic teammates Evelyne Hall and Jean Shiley; and good friend and protégée Betty Dodd. The book is thus sprinkled with reflections on both the life and athletic career of Associated Press's six-time Woman Athlete of the Year.

Schoor, Gene. BABE DIDRIKSON: THE WORLD'S GREATEST WOMAN ATHLETE. Garden City, N.Y.: Doubleday and Co., 1978. 185 p.

Schoor begins his biography of Babe Didrikson with the details of her National AAU championships in 1932 as a one-woman team. A brief chapter is devoted to her early childhood, but the major focus of the book is on her many and diverse accomplishments as a sports champion. A good bit of emphasis is also placed on her life and relationship with husband George Zaharias. The author paints a rather rosy picture of the life and career of Didrikson which some readers, who have read at length about her and followed her closely, may question. An appendix contains her championship records in track and golf.

Smith, Beatrice S. BABE: MILDRED DIDRIKSON ZAHARIAS. Milwaukee: Raintree Publications, 1976. 48 p.

This small volume for young readers outlines the sports career of Babe Didrikson Zaharias, often acclaimed the best woman athlete of all time. Her achievements in basketball, track, and golf, the activities in which she gained widespread attention, are described, as well as her return to championship status in golf after her first battle with cancer.

Part III

TECHNIQUES OF INSTRUCTION

A multitude of publications may be found that offer instructional techniques for every sport or sport-like activity in existence. Though the development of sports skills is essentially the same for either the male or female learner, many books have been written specifically for the woman in sport. This is particularly true in activities such as gymnastics in which rules or special equipment may differ for men and women. The recent increase in high-level sports competition for women has also resulted in publications which deal with the special concerns of training, conditioning and coaching the female athlete, who may need an emphasis different from that for men.

Chapter 6 includes books with instructional information for several different sports in one volume and books concerned with specific aspects of coaching women. Books in chapter 7 deal with single sports activities and include instructional techniques directed specifically toward female learners. Even though most volumes are titled as activities for women, much of the information is usable for either male or female.

Chapter 6

COLLECTED WORKS, TEACHING, AND COACHING

Broer, Marion R., ed. INDIVIDUAL SPORTS FOR WOMEN. 5th ed. Philadelphia: W.B. Saunders Co., 1971. 386 p.

> A section on principles of learning introduces this instructional
> manual for individual sports. Succeeding chapters cover archery,
> badminton, bowling, fencing, golf, riding, swimming, and tennis.
> Several different authors have contributed to the book, and each
> section covers skill analysis, suggested lessons, organizational tech-
> niques, and recommended equipment. A bibliography for further
> reading is included for each sport; for some activities, audio-
> visual materials are also listed.

Deatherage, Dorothy, and Reid, C. Patricia. ADMINISTRATION OF WOMEN'S
COMPETITIVE SPORTS. Dubuque, Iowa: William C. Brown Co., 1977. 255 p.
Paperbound.

> In addition to the mechanical aspects of administering competitive
> sports programs such as policies and procedures, public relations,
> coaching, and organization, the authors have considered the philo-
> sophic bases for the conduct of such programs for women. A sec-
> tion on the historical development of competitive sports for women
> is included, and a lengthy appendix provides samples of materials
> in current use for administrative purposes.

Miller, Donna Mae. COACHING THE FEMALE ATHLETE. Philadelphia: Lea
and Febiger, 1974. 212 p.

> The general nature of the title of this book suggests the content
> of its pages. Miller has made a broad, theoretical analysis of
> coaching the female athlete with no attempt to include the coach-
> ing needs of specific sports. She discusses motor-learning concepts,
> mechanical principles, training and conditioning procedures, and
> motivation techniques applicable to all sports. She also has at-
> tempted to provide a synthesis of the limited research conducted
> on the female athlete, particularly in the physiological and psy-
> chological areas.

Mushier, Carole L. TEAM SPORTS FOR GIRLS AND WOMEN. Dubuque, Iowa: William C. Brown and Co., 1973. 207 p.

This book focuses on teaching techniques for the team sports commonly included as activities in physical education programs for girls and women: basketball, field hockey, lacrosse, soccer, speedball, speed-a-way, softball, and volleyball. A chapter of general information on principles of learning applied to team sports precedes the chapters on specific techniques for each of the sports. Skill analysis, team strategy, necessary equipment, and a unit plan of instruction for beginning players are included for each activity. A brief bibliography concludes each sports chapter.

Neal, Patsy. COACHING METHODS FOR WOMEN. 2d ed. Reading, Mass.: Addison-Wesley Publishing Co., 1978. 281 p.

This book is written primarily for coaches of girls' and women's sports and includes chapters on the role of the coach, factors in coaching women, and prerequisites for champions as well as the practical aspects of coaching, such as organizing and selecting a team, training and conditioning, and planning for the sports season. Title IX of the 1972 Education Act is discussed in relation to athletic programs for women. A final chapter, more than half of the book, provides skill and strategy analyses and coaching suggestions for twelve different sports. Basketball is conspicuous by its absence; however, a prior publishing commitment prevented Neal's including it. The book offers diverse information concerning the coaching of women, and Neal's own philosophy of coaching is evident in many of the chapters.

Neal, Patsy, and Tutko, Thomas A. COACHING GIRLS AND WOMEN, PSYCHOLOGICAL PERSPECTIVES. Boston: Allyn and Bacon, 1975. 235 p.

Written by a female coach and former athlete and a male psychologist, this book provides unusual insight into the coaching of female athletes. Instead of the practical "how to" kinds of information for coaches, the authors have delved into the processes for understanding the woman coach and the woman athlete. The provocative chapter titles entice one to read further in the section on understanding the athlete: "Hassles and Hang-ups," "The Achievement-Oriented Female in American Society," "Why Play?" and "The Female Athlete in the Emotional Milieu of Sport." The final chapters, such as "The Personality of the Coach" and "Coaching the Superior Female Athlete," offer more practical advice, and excellent bibliographies are included with chapters throughout the book.

Paterson, Ann, and West, Eula, eds. TEAM SPORTS FOR GIRLS. 2d ed. New York: Ronald Press Co., 1971. 351 p.

This book is designed as an instructional manual for teaching team sports to girls. The eight sports included are basketball, field hockey, lacrosse, soccer, speedball, speed-a-way, softball, and volleyball. General information about the teaching of team sports is presented followed by separate chapters written by several different authors for each sport. These chapters include history and purpose of the game, necessary facilities and equipment, analysis of game skills, techniques of team strategy, and a suggested teaching progression.

Poindexter, Hally B.W., and Mushier, Carole L. COACHING COMPETITIVE TEAM SPORTS FOR GIRLS AND WOMEN. Philadelphia: W.B. Saunders Co., 1973. 244 p.

The authors of this book have attempted to provide an overall view of the information needed by coaches of women's team sports. An introductory chapter defines the role of competition, its purposes, objectives, and values for women. Subsequent chapters provide practical information concerning the organization and administration of a competitive program and guidelines for team selection and practice sessions. Separate chapters on basketball, field hockey, lacrosse, softball, and volleyball provide specific suggestions for coaching each of these sports. Topics covered include player selection, advanced skills necessary for competitive play, team strategy, suggestions for practice sessions, and coaching during game play.

Vannier, Maryhelen, and Poindexter, Hally B.W. INDIVIDUAL AND TEAM SPORTS FOR GIRLS AND WOMEN. 3d ed. Philadelphia: W.B. Saunders Co., 1976. 762 p.

The primary purpose of this book is to provide instructional information for most individual and team sports taught in school physical education programs. Each sports section contains skill analyses, suggested teaching units, class organization, skills progression, and facilities and equipment needed for the sport. Separate chapters on the unique contributions of sports to life, principles of motor learning, class organization and management, and competition offer general information for the conduct of sports classes. A special feature of the book is the inclusion of suggested readings, audiovisual materials, and periodicals for each of the sports.

Chapter 7

INSTRUCTION FOR WOMEN IN SPECIFIC SPORTS

BASKETBALL

Barnes, Mildred J. WOMEN'S BASKETBALL. Boston: Allyn and Bacon, 1972. 328 p.

> This book was written at the time of the transition from the six-player to five-player game for women. Barnes provides detailed analyses of individual skills and offensive and defensive strategies for the five-player game. She concludes with teaching progressions, suggestions for class organization, and ideas for use by coaches working with competitive teams.

Bell, Mary M. WOMEN'S BASKETBALL. 2d ed. Dubuque, Iowa: William C. Brown Co., 1973. 132 p.

> A brief history of basketball introduces this book. Defensive and offensive skills and strategies are analyzed, and suggestions for coaching competitive teams conclude the volume.

Ebert, Frances H., and Cheatum, Billye Ann. BASKETBALL. 2d ed. Philadelphia: W.B. Saunders Co., 1977. 282 p. Paperbound.

> In addition to analyses of individual skills and team strategies, this book includes sections on conditioning for basketball, treatment of injuries to athletes, and suggestions for coaching competitive teams. Although the first edition of this book, BASKETBALL --FIVE PLAYERS (1972) was written for women, in this edition the authors have attempted to consider play for both men's and women's teams. Content does seem to be directed primarily toward women players, however.

Lowry, Carla. WOMEN'S BASKETBALL. Chicago: Athletic Institute, 1972. 68 p.

> This book briefly describes techniques and strategies for playing basketball, but is illustrated with numerous photographs depicting information covered in the text.

Miller, Kenneth D., and Horky, Rita J. MODERN BASKETBALL FOR WOMEN. Columbus, Ohio: Charles E. Merrill Publishing Co., 1970. 182 p. Paperbound.

> A brief history of women's basketball, including a section on international competition, introduces this book for teachers and coaches. Published just prior to the introduction of the five-player game in schools and colleges, the book covers techniques for both the five-player and the six-player game. Fundamental skills of the game are analyzed, and basic offensive and defensive strategies are described. A final section offers suggestions for problems which may be encountered by the beginning coach.

Rush, Cathy, and Mifflin, Lowrie. WOMEN'S BASKETBALL. New York: Hawthorn Books, 1976. 124 p.

> Written by the coach of the Immaculata College team that won three national collegiate championships, this book is directed toward the person interested in learning basketball. Rush utilizes the technique of "talking to" the reader as she describes the components that develop a strong player--attitudes, conditioning, basic skills, and offensive and defensive tactics.

Stutts, Ann. WOMEN'S BASKETBALL. Pacific Palisades, Calif.: Goodyear Publishing Co., 1973. 82 p. Paperbound.

> A brief history of basketball for women introduces this book which is devoted primarily to techniques for playing the game. Skills and strategies are analyzed, and a brief synopsis of rules for women is included.

Turnbull, Anne E. BASKETBALL FOR WOMEN. Reading, Mass.: Addison-Wesley Publishing Co., 1973. 211 p. Paperbound.

> Although this book contains skill analyses and descriptions of offensive and defensive strategy, it is primarily concerned with other facets which should be helpful to the coaches of competitive teams. Such topics covered by the author are administrative procedures, conditioning, prevention of simple athletic injuries, and psychological aspects of coaching. Each of the nine chapters concludes with selected references.

Warren, William E. TEAM PATTERNS IN GIRLS' AND WOMEN'S BASKETBALL. New York: A.S. Barnes and Co., 1976. 240 p.

> This book is devoted entirely to offensive and defensive strategies for women's basketball. It is unique in that all material deals with the six-player game, which is still played in only a few states at the high school level, rather than the five-player game, which is now almost universally played by girls and women.

FIELD HOCKEY AND LACROSSE

Barnes, Mildred J. FIELD HOCKEY, THE COACH AND THE PLAYER. Boston: Allyn and Bacon, 1969. 262 p.

Almost every aspect needed for playing, teaching, or coaching field hockey is covered in this book. Skill analysis, game strategy, practice suggestions, rainy-day ideas, introducing the game to beginners, facilities and equipment, and coaching are presented. Sections on position play and coaching were written by members of the United States Team, players selected from regional teams to make up the National Team.

Brackenridge, Celia. WOMEN'S LACROSSE. Woodbury, N.Y.: Barron's Educational Series, 1978.

Detailed analysis of fundamental skills makes this an excellent resource book for the beginning lacrosse learner. Offensive and defensive strategy is discussed in a limited way, since lacrosse is primarily a game of creativity rather than "set" plays. A concluding chapter suggests ideas for effective use of practice time.

Bryant, Carol A. HOCKEY FOR SCHOOLS. London: Pelman Books, 1969. 164 p.

The title of this book is indicative of its content. Individual techniques are analyzed and team strategy is described, but a special feature is the author's emphasis on choosing the right movement at the right time. Sections on umpiring, tournament organization, equipment, and maintenance of grounds provide additional information for the hockey teacher.

Delano, Anne Lee. LACROSSE FOR GIRLS AND WOMEN. Dubuque, Iowa: William C. Brown Co., 1970. 76 p. Paperbound.

In this basic instructional manual the author covers skill techniques, requirements for team positions, and fundamental offensive and defensive play. "The Lore of Lacrosse" briefly traces the history of the game, and a summary of rules clarifies game play.

Flint, Rachel Heywood. FIELD HOCKEY. Woodbury, N.Y.: Barron's Educational Series, 1978. 64 p.

Basic skills, tactics, and rules for play are covered in this easily readable book written for the beginning hockey player.

Haussermann, Caroline. FIELD HOCKEY. Boston: Allyn and Bacon, 1970. 77 p.

The basic fundamentals of field hockey are presented in this book. The author uses a conceptual approach in developing the informational materials and provides experiences for learning the concepts selected.

Hickey, Melvyn. HOCKEY FOR WOMEN. 2d ed. London: Kaye and Ward, 1970. 112 p.

The author of this book, a former international hockey player herself, directs her information to the player learning the game. Individual skills, team tactics, and player responsibilities are simply described for the reader.

Kurtz, Agnes B. WOMEN'S LACROSSE, FOR COACHES AND PLAYERS. Hanover, N.H.: ABK Publications, 1977. 132 p. Paperbound.

Since this book was written primarily for use by coaches, the major portion is devoted to advanced skills and strategies. Fundamental skills are analyzed, however, and a history of lacrosse is included. In a special section on techniques of coaching, the author discusses conditioning, assessing the players and the game, and psychological factors. She concludes with a resume of the rules of the game.

Lees, Josephine T., and Shellenberger, Josephine. FIELD HOCKEY. New York: Ronald Press Co., 1969. 147 p.

Equipment, individual skills, team tactics, umpiring, duties of players, and practice procedures are covered in this book written for the hockey teacher. The authors conclude with a lengthy glossary of field hockey terms.

Read, Brenda. BETTER HOCKEY FOR GIRLS. London: Kaye and Ward, 1976. 95 p.

Material in this book is presented in a manner usable by the beginning hockey player. Skills and techniques are clearly described, and a special section gives hints for developing skillful play.

Read, Brenda, and Walker, Freda. ADVANCED HOCKEY FOR WOMEN. London: Faber and Faber, 1976. 166 p.

The authors of this book have focused on material precisely described by the title, advanced hockey. They have omitted the usual beginning skill analyses and team offense and defense and directed their attention to more advanced skills, assessing opponents' play, tactical possibilities from set plays, and plays usable in unorthodox situations.

Spencer, Helen. BEGINNING FIELD HOCKEY. Belmont, Calif.: Wadsworth Publishing Co., 1970. 61 p. Paperbound.

This book is written for the beginner; it includes a brief history of

hockey, rules for play, and analysis of individual skills. A final
section describes techniques for self-testing and evaluation.

Weir, Marie. HOCKEY COACHING, A PSYCHOLOGICAL APPROACH TO
THE WOMEN'S GAME. London: Kaye and Ward, 1977. 187 p.

The author departs from the usual skill and strategy analysis found
in many sport books and directs her attention to coaching hockey
and the application of psychological theories in that setting. The
content ranges from such topics as players' needs, team selection,
and role of the captain to the implications of an all-female squad,
coach-player relationships, group dynamics, and aggression in
hockey.

_____. WOMEN'S HOCKEY FOR THE SEVENTIES. London: Kaye and Ward,
1974. 190 p.

Although Weir provides information concerning skill performance
and game strategy, she goes beyond the usual sports instructional
manual to include principles of play, game psychology, suggestions
for coaching, and a look at the future of hockey for women.

Williams, Lee Ann. BASIC FIELD HOCKEY STRATEGY. Garden City, N.Y.:
Doubleday and Co., 1978. 105 p.

Williams discusses individual skills, defensive and offensive strategies, game rules, practice drills, and conditioning. Although a
brief section on advanced strategy is included, the book is essentially an introduction to field hockey for young players.

GOLF

Berg, Patty, with Schiewe, Marsh. INSIDE GOLF FOR WOMEN. Chicago:
Contemporary Books, 1977. 86 p.

A step-by-step analysis of the skills of golf is provided in this
book along with practice suggestions for improving one's game.
Berg also offers advice for some of the difficult situations encountered in the game such as playing out of sand traps and uphill
or sidehill shots.

Coyne, John, ed. THE NEW GOLF FOR WOMEN. New York: Doubleday
and Co., 1973. 223 p.

Each of the chapters in this book is authored by a professional
woman golfer writing in an area of the game in which she is considered outstanding. Kathy Whitworth analyzes fundamental skills.
Betty Burfeindt discusses driving for distance; Judy Rankin, playing
the woods; Sandy Haynie, playing the long irons; Sandy Palmer,
playing the short irons; and Mary Mills, playing the wedge. Put-

ting is analyzed by Pam Barnett, and Jane Blalock offers advice for playing trouble shots. The book is generously illustrated with photographs of the authors.

Haynie, Sandra. GOLF: A NATURAL COURSE FOR WOMEN. New York: Atheneum, 1975. 208 p.

Believing that all women have the timing, body control, and natural grace to learn golf and enjoy it, professional golfer Haynie attempts to provide the ingredients that will lead to learning and enjoyment. She offers suggestions for conditioning, tips on perfecting and improving performance, selecting appropriate equipment, and also provides ideas about how to look, what to wear, and how to act on the course. The book takes a somewhat different and refreshing approach from the usual instructional manual.

Moran, Sharron. GOLF IS A WOMAN'S GAME. New York: Hawthorn Books, 1971. 202 p.

Moran analyzes and illustrates with photographs the techniques of driving and putting the ball and offers suggestions for dealing with difficult shots. She describes each of the clubs and their uses, and in a section titled "Golf Clinic," she analyzes common performance problems and provides suggestions for improvement. A long list of golf terms is detailed and complete.

Saunders, Vivien. THE COMPLETE WOMAN GOLFER. London: Stanley Paul and Co., 1975. 144 p.

This book is written for beginning golfers and uses nontechnical language in analyzing golf skills and suggesting strategies for difficult strokes. Advice for selecting equipment is included, and the book concludes with a detailed glossary of golf terms.

GYMNASTICS

Bowers, Carolyn O.; Fie, Jacquelyn U.; Kjeldsen, Kitty; and Schmid, Andrea B. JUDGING AND COACHING WOMEN'S GYMNASTICS. Palo Alto, Calif.: National Press Books, 1972. 217 p.

This book was written to provide judges with a technical understanding of gymnastic skills and aid them in making the critical decisions necessary for judging competition. Good technique and common technical errors are described for each event, and specific penalties and deductions resulting in loss of points are listed. Other sections cover psychology of coaching and philosophy of judging and coaching gymnastics.

Carter, Ernestine Russell. GYMNASTICS FOR GIRLS AND WOMEN. Englewood Cliffs, N.J.: Prentice-Hall, 1969. 180 p.

This book is designed for the teacher of gymnastics. The skills most commonly performed in floor exercise, in vaulting, on the balance beam, and on the uneven bars are analyzed. Techniques of spotting and points of form are provided along with suggestions for judging performance and conducting a gymnastics meet.

Cochrane, Tuovi Sappinen. INTERNATIONAL GYMNASTICS FOR GIRLS AND WOMEN. Reading, Mass.: Addison-Wesley Publishing Co., 1969. 248 p.

Directed toward the gymnastics teacher, this book contains most of the information needed to begin a program. In addition to analysis of skills for the four competitive events, uneven bars, balance beam, floor exercise, and vaulting, the author has sections on gymnastics with instruments and hand apparatus, developmental exercises, and gymnastic routines. Sample lessons are provided for some of the activities.

Cooper, Phyllis. FEMININE GYMNASTICS. 2d ed. Minneapolis: Burgess Publishing Co., 1973. 250 p.

An instructional manual for teachers, this book includes skill analysis, spotting techniques, teaching methods, evaluation procedures, and errors most commonly made by students. Skills for the four competitive events, floor exercise, uneven bars, vaulting, and balance beam, are described as well as tumbling and trampoline skills. The book is amply illustrated with more than 300 drawings.

Coulton, Jill. WOMEN'S GYMNASTICS. Wakefield, West Yorkshire, Engl.: E.P. Publishing, 1977. 116 p.

This instructional manual written by a senior coach of the British Amateur Gymnastics Association includes skill analysis for performing the competitive events for women--beam, horse, bars, and floor exercise. Instructions are brief and simple, but are profusely illustrated with photographs and diagrams. A complete series of basic exercises is suggested as a guide for warm-up activities. Although the book does not include spotting techniques used in the early phases of learning skills, the succinct analyses of skills and excellent illustrations should be useful to the teacher-coach.

Drury, Blanche Jessen, and Schmid, Andrea B. INTRODUCTION TO WOMEN'S GYMNASTICS. Palo Alto, Calif.: National Press Books, 1973. 112 p.

This book was written primarily for the beginning gymnastics student and the secondary school teacher. Skills for each of the competitive events, balance beam, uneven bars, floor exercise, and vaulting, are analyzed along with basic tumbling and dance moves. A skills progression check list is included for the four competitive events.

Fidler, Janet, and Steele, Brian. OLYMPIC GYMNASTICS FOR GIRLS.
Altrincham, Engl.: John Sherratt and Son, 1976. 128 p. Paperbound.

Skills for each of the four competitive events, vaulting, balance
beam, uneven bars, and floor exercise, are analyzed for the
teacher of gymnastics. Warm-up activities for general class use
are described, and numerous photographs illustrate appropriate
spotting techniques for many of the skills.

Gault, Jim, with Grant, Jack. THE WORLD OF WOMEN'S GYMNASTICS.
Millbrae, Calif.: Celestial Arts, 1976. 141 p. Paperbound.

Using an informal and personal approach to writing, Gault explores
the many facets of the sport of gymnastics outside the realm of
skill analysis. He considers the mental and emotional attitudes
necessary for success; the influence of parents in gymnastic training; the problems and pitfalls of the international gymnastic judge;
and some of the political aspects evident in the 1976 Olympic
gymnastics competition.

Hughes, Eric, ed. GYMNASTICS FOR GIRLS. 2d ed. New York: Ronald
Press Co., 1971. 320 p.

This book was designed to be a teaching guide for physical edu-
cators and coaches. In addition to analysis of gymnastic skills,
safety practices, teaching hints, and rules for each event are also
described. A special feature is a chapter on "modern" or rhythmic
gymnastics in which performers use balls, hoops, ribbons, and ropes
in their routines.

Ito, Robert, and Dolney, Pam Chilla. MASTERING WOMEN'S GYMNASTICS.
Chicago: Contemporary Books, 1978. 160 p. Paperbound.

This instructional manual provides the reader with an overall view
of the requirements for the sport of gymnastics. Exercises and
fundamental skills for "warming up" are followed by analysis of
skills for the four competitive events for women--floor exercise,
vaulting, balance beam, and uneven bars. Sequential photographs
and drawings are amply used to illustrate the skills. Spotting
techniques are described and also illustrated throughout the text.
A detailed glossary of gymnastic terms concludes the book which
should be useful to both students and teachers.

Johnson, Barry L., and Boudreaux, Patricia D. BASIC GYMNASTICS FOR
GIRLS AND WOMEN. New York: Appleton-Century-Crofts, 1971. 130 p.
Paperbound.

The title of this book aptly describes it. It is a book for beginning learners, but may be utilized by the teacher of beginning
classes. Approximately one hundred stunts are presented, and the
final sections give suggestions for class organization and evaluating
and grading students.

Kjeldsen, Kitty. WOMEN'S GYMNASTICS. 2d ed. Boston: Allyn and Bacon, 1975. 92 p. Paperbound.

> A simplified analysis of basic skills is combined with a movement-exploration approach to aid learners in mastering beginning gymnastic skills. Key concepts around which gymnastics is structured have been identified, and learning experiences are suggested for developing specific outcomes.

Murray, Mimi. WOMEN'S GYMNASTICS. Boston: Allyn and Bacon, 1979. 289 p.

> This book, written by the coach of three National Championship Women's Gymnastics teams, offers a comprehensive view of gymnastics for women. Chapters for each competitive event provide skill analysis, teaching techniques, skill progressions, and corrections for common errors for each event. A separate chapter examines the coaching role and offers special advice for the person in that position. The book is well illustrated with both photographs and drawings, and information throughout the book covers basic as well as advanced skill levels.

Ryan, Frank. GYMNASTICS FOR GIRLS. New York: Viking Press, 1976. 431 p.

> The major content of this book is photographs. Over 200 skills for the four competitive gymnastic events for women are briefly described, and two to seven progressive photographs illustrate the performance of each skill.

Schmid, Andrea B. MODERN RHYTHMIC GYMNASTICS. Palo Alto, Calif.: Mayfield Publishing Co., 1976. 379 p.

> Teachers of rhythmic gymnastics will find this book complete and detailed. A history of the activity clarifies the differences between this and other forms of gymnastics. Other sections provide analysis of skills using balls, ropes, hoops, ribbons, clubs, scarves, flags, and wands. Descriptions of basic dance movements and movement combinations with the hand apparatus complete the instructional information for this area of gymnastics.

Schmid, Andrea B., and Drury, Blanche J[essen]. GYMNASTICS FOR WOMEN. 4th ed. Palo Alto, Calif.: Mayfield Publishing Co., 1977. 396 p. Paperbound.

> A brief résumé of the history of gymnastics for women in the United States introduces this instructional manual for teachers and coaches. Some 200 skills performed in the four competitive events are analyzed, and teaching suggestions and safety measures are described throughout the different sections. A separate section deals with modern rhythmic gymnastics, and judging techniques conclude the volume.

Schreiber, Mary L. WOMEN'S GYMNASTICS. Pacific Palisades, Calif.: Goodyear Publishing Co., 1969. 88 p. Paperbound.

> Basic skills for each of the major gymnastic events for women are briefly analyzed in this book for beginning learners, and conditioning exercises are suggested. Sequence photographs illustrate most of the basic skills.

Sullivan, George. BETTER GYMNASTICS FOR GIRLS. New York: Dodd, Mead and Co., 1977. 62 p.

> A brief history of gymnastics introduces this book for the beginning gymnast, and most of the remaining text is devoted to simple instructions for the basic skills in the four women's gymnastic events. Photographs, all of young gymnasts, illustrate the techniques of floor exercise, vaulting, the balance beam, and the uneven bars. Though not written in extremely simple language, the content of the book is directed toward the young reader.

Wachtel, Erna, and Loken, Newton C. GIRLS' GYMNASTICS. New York: Sterling Publishing Co., 1977. 94 p.

> Basic techniques for girls' gymnastics are analyzed in this book, and each analysis is illustrated with photographs. In addition to the four competitive events for women, balance beam, uneven bars, vaulting, and floor exercise, techniques for the even parallel bars are also included.

Warren, Meg. THE BOOK OF GYMNASTICS. London: Arthur Barker, 1972. 106 p.

> Technique and style for performing basic skills in the major gymnastic events for women are described in this book for beginning learners. The information is easily understood and will be of greatest interest to persons just beginning to work on gymnastic skills.

MARTIAL ARTS AND SELF-DEFENSE

Cahill, Willy. KICK AND RUN, SELF DEFENSE FOR WOMEN. Burbank, Calif.: Ohara Publications, 1977. 95 p. Paperbound.

> Basic fundamentals for self-protection are simply analyzed and illustrated with photographs in this book, written for the person who may not have time for instructional classes. The title is indicative of the content, as most of the techniques are kicking skills, but striking skills, breaking holds, and handling common attack situations receive some attention. The book cannot be considered an in-depth study of self-defense but rather a presentation of basic techniques which may be self-taught.

Conroy, Mary. THE RATIONAL WOMAN'S GUIDE TO SELF-DEFENSE. New York: Grosset and Dunlap, 1975. 128 p. Paperbound.

This book begins with basic self-defense strategies and a long list of suggestions for avoiding confrontation. Basic techniques of kicking, striking, and releases from assailants' holds are described and illustrated and followed by suggestions for using simple weapons and precautions necessary in their use. A separate section discusses rape and what to do in case of such an occurrence. Special emphasis is placed on reporting the crime and follow-up procedures.

Gardner, Ruth. JUDO FOR THE GENTLE WOMAN. Rutland, Vt.: C.E. Tuttle Co., 1971. 147 p.

The basic fundamentals of judo, for which some schools award a "green-belt" degree, are included in this book. Falls, self-defense techniques, and basic throwing techniques are analyzed and illustrated with photographs. The book is designed as a "how-to-do-it" book; however, the author stresses the importance of a competent instructor in actual practice and for progressing to more advanced skills.

Gustuson, Donald L., and Masaki, Linda. SELF-DEFENSE FOR WOMEN. Boston: Allyn and Bacon, 1970. 80 p.

This book is designed for use in instructional classes or by the self-learner and utilizes a conceptual approach in presenting the material. Basic concepts are followed by related information and practice situations for developing the appropriate skills and knowledge necessary for defending oneself.

Heyden, Margaret S., and Tarpenning, Allan. PERSONAL DEFENSE FOR WOMEN. Belmont, Calif.: Wadsworth Publishing Co., 1970. 94 p.

Basic techniques for self-defense for a variety of situations are described by the authors. Other chapters discuss equipment, such as a comb or nail file, which might be available to a woman for defending herself, safety precautions to avoid problems, legal implications of defense, and training to keep in shape. Coverage for most subjects is cursory except the section on techniques, which is covered in more detail.

Luchsinger, Judith A.H. PRACTICAL SELF-DEFENSE FOR WOMEN. Minneapolis: Dillon Press, 1977. 78 p. Paperbound.

Utilizing her background and experience in judo, the author suggests basic techniques for protection from assault. Pressure points and vulnerable areas are described, as well as techniques for escaping from an assailant, falling, and throwing an attacker. Separate sections are devoted to suggestions for preventing attack and developing a mental preparedness for self-protection. The practicality of some of the techniques included, such as advanced throwing techniques, is questionable, and the author's lack of current information is evident when she states that almost no written instructions on the subject of self-defense for women are available (p. 7).

Neff, Fred. SELF-PROTECTION GUIDEBOOK FOR GIRLS AND WOMEN. Minneapolis: Lerner Publications Co., 1977. 63 p.

Suggestions for avoiding potential trouble introduce this manual of basic self-defense techniques. Each of the skills is then presented in a simple series of learning steps. Fighting stances for self-protection, defending against attack with blocks, punches, and kicks, and escaping from attack are described. A final section reviews briefly the key points of self-protection.

Offstein, Jerrold. SELF-DEFENSE FOR WOMEN. Palo Alto, Calif.: National Press Books, 1972. 76 p. Paperbound.

Using elements and techniques from karate, jiujitsu, judo, and aikido, Offstein has developed a progressive series of skills for practical self-defense. The tactics are designed primarily for repelling sexual assaults but may, of course, be useful in other situations. A rather lengthy section of the book discusses history, philosophy, and principles of karate since the author believes this background is basic to successful performance of the techniques he describes.

Pirnat, Janet Wenger. PERSONAL DEFENCE SKILLS FOR WOMEN. Champaign, Ill.: Stipes Publishing Co., 1975. 111 p. Paperbound.

Designed for use in either a teacher-directed class or by the self-learner, this book covers personal defense skills for a variety of different types of physical attack. The book is organized into units of basic and advanced defensive skills, and each unit is structured in ten progressive lessons. Skills are analyzed, common errors described, and evaluation techniques presented, and a series of photographs illustrates each skill.

Sugano, Jun. KARATE AND SELF-DEFENSE FOR WOMEN. London: Ward Lock, 1976. 119 p.

Basic fundamentals of karate are analyzed and fully illustrated with photographs in this book. Drawing from those basic skills, the author presents techniques of self-defense for a variety of possibly dangerous situations. A final chapter suggests a series of calisthenics for developing flexibility and stamina, and improving concentration and control of power as a basis for becoming more capable of self-protection.

Tegner, Bruce, and McGrath, Alice. SELF-DEFENSE AND ASSAULT PREVEN-TION FOR GIRLS AND WOMEN. Ventura, Calif.: Thor Publishing Co., 1977. 125 p.

> In a book designed for and first used by physical education teach-ers, the authors have outlined a step-by-step procedure for learning self-defense techniques for a variety of situations. They conclude this teaching manual with suggestions for preventing situations in which assault could occur.

SOFTBALL

Claflin, Edward. THE IRRESISTIBLE AMERICAN SOFTBALL BOOK. Garden City, N.Y.: Doubleday and Co., 1978. 128 p. Paperbound.

> With such provocative chapter titles as "Softball Power," "Under-hand Combat," and "I'll Flip You for Shifty," Claflin weaves an interesting story with factual information about the game of soft-ball. The fundamental skills of pitching, catching, batting, and fielding are described, but the bulk of information deals with other aspects of the game. Topics such as amateur and professional soft-ball, senior citizen players, actors and politicians who play soft-ball, and little known facts about the game are included. Some information about women in softball is interwoven throughout the book, but the chapter, "Women's Clout," describes the establish-ment of the professional All-American Girls Softball League in 1943 and a brief sketch of the career of pitcher Joan Joyce. Short background and record data are provided for ten women who have been elected to the American Softball Association's Hall of Fame.

Dobson, Margaret J., and Sisley, Becky L. SOFTBALL FOR GIRLS. New York: Ronald Press Co., 1971. 224 p.

> A history of softball introduces this book written for teachers and coaches of the game. Virtually all phases of softball are covered from basic skill analysis to advanced playing and coaching tech-niques. Evaluation techniques, indoor and outdoor practice situa-tions, and suggestions for elementary, secondary, and college programs are provided for the teacher. A bibliography of addi-tional sources for softball and a list of visual aids offer further information for the reader.

Jones, Billie J., and Murray, Mary Jo. SOFTBALL: CONCEPTS FOR TEACH-ERS AND COACHES. Dubuque, Iowa: William C. Brown Co., 1978. 215 p. Paperbound.

> The authors have provided detailed information on softball in this book for teachers and coaches. A history of softball is presented, and the slow-pitch and fast-pitch games are defined. In the chap-ters on skill analysis and offensive and defensive strategies, basic

concepts are listed, followed by key points related to the concepts. Each section, such as "The First Baseman" and "The Outfield," concludes with practice drills and teaching-learning tips for that specialized area. Detailed advice for the purchase and care of equipment and uniforms is offered, and chapters on conditioning, teaching, and coaching complete this book. Though designed for use by either women or men, most of the photographs used for illustration are of women.

Joyce, Joan, and Anquillan, John. WINNING SOFTBALL. Chicago: Henry Regnery Co., 1975. 109 p.

This book, coauthored by Joan Joyce, the "Babe Ruth of women's softball" and considered to be the best female pitcher in the sport, is usable by both men and women. The basic skills of pitching, batting, and fielding are analyzed, and conditioning techniques for the player are included. A brief section compares the men's and women's game, and a final chapter clarifies the differences between the fast-pitch game and the slow-pitch game which seems to be increasing in popularity.

Kneer, Marian E., and McCord, Charles L. SOFTBALL: SLOW AND FAST PITCH. 2d ed. Dubuque, Iowa: William C. Brown Co. Publishers, 1976. 96 p. Paperbound.

This book, written for use by either women or men, departs from the usual format for such instructional manuals. Each chapter and sections within some chapters begin with instructional objectives which identify the content which follows, and self-evaluation questions are interspersed throughout the book to help the reader determine attainment of the stated objectives. The material covered includes offensive and defensive skills and patterns of play, language and lore of the game, rules, selection and care of equipment, suggestions for teacher and coach, and a brief section on conditioning and competitive play. The book is directed primarily toward the student of softball interested in self-learning.

Littlewood, Mary. WOMEN'S SOFTBALL. Chicago: Athletic Institute, 1971. 76 p.

Fundamental skills needed for playing fast-pitch softball are described and illustrated with photographs and diagrams. The special responsibilities of infield and outfield players are outlined, and a detailed glossary of softball terms concludes this book for the beginning player.

Walsh, Loren. CONTEMPORARY SOFTBALL. Chicago: Contemporary Books, 1978. 122 p.

This book begins with a history of softball and the differences in the fast- and slow-pitch games. The remaining chapters cover basic skills and strategies necessary for playing the game: infield basics and strategy, the outfielder, pitching and catching, and hitting and running. A detailed glossary concludes the volume, and illustrations throughout are of both males and females.

TRACK AND FIELD AND RUNNING

Benyo, Rich, ed. THE COMPLETE WOMAN RUNNER. Mountain View, Calif.: World Publications, 1978. 443 p.

Several authors have contributed to what does appear to be a "complete" book of running for women. Chapters devoted to training, dealing with a family, safety for female runners, injury prevention, psychology of competition, coaching for women, anatomical, cardiorespiratory, and psychological aspects of running, and progressing beyond jogging, cover virtually everything on aspiring runner may wish to know. A short history of running provides an overview of women's long-distance running; brief profiles of Roberta Gibb, Kathy Switzer, Nina Kuscsik, and Sara Berman describe their pioneering efforts in the sport. Brief sketches are also included for fifty American women who run--the "average" runners who may train a minimum of a mile and a half per day to those who run one hundred miles a week. The book is a practical guide for the woman just starting to run or who may want to make running a vital part of her life.

Costanza, Betty, with Glossbrenner, Alfred. WOMEN'S TRACK AND FIELD. New York: Hawthorn Books, 1978. 163 p. Paperbound.

The content of this book is directed primarily toward the beginning athlete and written in a style that could be used for self-learning. Detailed mechanical analyses have been omitted; however, sufficient information is provided for learning acceptable performance. Techniques for warming up and proper conditioning are also included.

Foreman, Ken, and Husted, Virginia. TRACK AND FIELD TECHNIQUES FOR GIRLS AND WOMEN. 3d ed. Dubuque, Iowa: William C. Brown Co., 1977. 287 p. Paperbound.

The major track and field events in which women participate are analyzed in this book, and progressive training schedules for each event are outlined. Guidelines for planning and conducting a track and field meet offer helpful assistance to the novice meet director.

Jackson, Nell C. TRACK AND FIELD FOR GIRLS AND WOMEN. Minneapolis: Burgess Publishing Co., 1969. 143 p.

Former Olympic competitor and coach Jackson has utilized her own past experiences and knowledge in analyzing the major track and

and field events of running, throwing, and jumping. Both photographs and drawings are used to illustrate the mechanical principles
described in the text. Separate sections on conditioning and training, warming up, and organizing a track and field meet are also
included.

Lance, Kathryn. RUNNING FOR HEALTH AND BEAUTY. Indianapolis: Bobbs-
Merrill Co., 1977. 193 p. Paperbound.

This complete guide for the woman runner provides detailed information for the woman who wants to begin a running program.
What to wear, where and when to run, techniques of running,
running injuries and how to avoid them, and advice for "getting
started" are described by the author. A section "for women only"
deals with special aspects of women's running: menstruation, pregnancy, older women, and dangers faced by women, especially in
running after dark. In a final chapter the author writes about
long-distance competitive running for women.

Miller, Kenneth D., and Jones, Billie J. TRACK AND FIELD FOR GIRLS.
New York: Ronald Press Co., 1974. 157 p.

The authors of this book begin with a brief résumé of the history
of track and field for women, particularly in relation to the modern Olympic Games, and provide further historical highlights for
individual events in the introductions to succeeding chapters. Performance techniques for all major events including the baseball
and basketball throws are presented, and the book concludes with
sections on planning a meet and suggestions for coaching.

Paish, Wilf, and Duffy, Tony. ATHLETICS IN FOCUS. London: Lepus Books,
1976. 163 p.

This book captures the essence of track and field athletics through
the eye of the camera. Technical information is minimal, and
about half of the ninety-two illustrations included are photographs
of women.

Parker, Virginia, and Kennedy, Robert. TRACK AND FIELD FOR GIRLS AND
WOMEN. Philadelphia: W.B. Saunders Co., 1969. 115 p.

This book is written primarily for the track and field participant
who wishes to learn basic skills or improve performance by cor-
recting common errors. No attempt is made to provide a detailed
mechanical analysis of events; however, sufficient information for
effective performance of fundamental skills in the various events
is included. The authors also provide a brief section on training
and conditioning techniques.

Runner's World Magazine. THE FEMALE RUNNER. Mountain View, Calif.:
World Publications, 1974. 31 p.

The editors of this book have compiled a collection of articles concerned with the female runner. Divided, into four short sections, the book considers "Prospects"--what the future holds for women runners; "Mythology"--an attempt to dispel the myths about the female athlete; "Physiology"--some of the special aspects of training related to women; and "Psychology"--some of the psychological dimensions of the woman who chooses to be an athlete.

Stephens, Will. WOMEN'S TRACK AND FIELD. Chicago: Athletic Institute, 1973. 92 p. Paperbound.

Performance analysis for each of the women's track and field events is outlined and fully illustrated with photographs. A brief résumé of simplified rules and diet suggestions for women track athletes is included.

Thompson, Donnis H. MODERN TRACK AND FIELD FOR GIRLS AND WOMEN. Boston: Allyn and Bacon, 1973. 274 p.

The mechanical principles of performance for each of the major track and field events are presented in this book along with common errors and corrections, a teaching progression, and rules that govern participation in each event. A separate section offers planning suggestions for teaching and coaching track and field, and organizational and administrative procedures for planning meets.

_____. WOMEN'S TRACK AND FIELD. Boston: Allyn and Bacon, 1969. 86 p.

This book is designed in a manner which allows the reader to learn the activities through self-instruction. Major concepts about the skills are identified, and selected learning experiences leading to an understanding of those concepts are presented. Techniques for performing each of the events in which women participate are included.

Tyus, Wyomia. INSIDE JOGGING FOR WOMEN. Chicago: Contemporary Books, 1978. 60 p.

Former Olympic runner Tyus has written this book for the general reader interested in running as exercise for fitness rather than competitive running. She describes the basics of beginning a jogging program and techniques for running, and concludes with a section on running as a source of happiness.

Ullyot, Joan. WOMEN'S RUNNING. Mountain View, Calif.: World Publications, 1976. 153 p. Paperbound.

This book, authored by a medical doctor and marathon runner, offers detailed information to the woman interested in running either for health and fitness or for racing. She includes basic principles

such as shoes and clothing, warm-up, and safety as well as physiological aspects of running and information related to women
only, such as running during the menstrual period or pregnancy.
Three sections are devoted specifically to techniques for beginners,
intermediates, and racers, and the author makes a careful distinc-
tion between running for fitness and running in competition.

Wakefield, Frances; Harkins, Dorothy; and Cooper, John M. TRACK AND
FIELD FUNDAMENTALS FOR GIRLS AND WOMEN. St. Louis: C.V. Mosby
Co., 1973. 295 p.

This book is designed as a basic text for the teaching of track and
field events. Not only does it include an analysis of the techniques of performance, but teaching progressions, training suggestions, officiating techniques, and meet planning are also detailed.
An unusual feature is the chapter on improving equipment when
standard equipment is not available.

Wilt, Fred; Ecker, Tom; and Hay, Jim, eds. CHAMPIONSHIP TRACK AND
FIELD FOR WOMEN. West Nyack, N.Y.: Parker Publishing Co., 1978.
270 p.

An analysis of each of the nine track and field events in which
women participate has been written by a contributor recognized
for his or her expertise in that event. Other chapters consider
the biomechanical, physiological, and sociopsychological aspects
of the female competitor. The book focuses on coaching techniques
for skilled performers but presents a range of information from fundamental techniques to advanced technical knowledge.

VOLLEYBALL

Peppler, Mary Jo. INSIDE VOLLEYBALL FOR WOMEN. Chicago: Henry
Regnery Co., 1977. 90 p.

Writing in an informal, sometimes humorous style, Peppler has designed this book not only to help the beginning volleyball player
develop skill but also to develop the right "mind-set" needed to
become a competitive player. In addition to analysis of the techniques of volleyball, she has chapters on becoming a volleyball
player, winning, and the nature of the game. Throughout the
book she consistently directs encouraging comments to the reader.

Schaafsma, Frances, and Heck, Ann. VOLLEYBALL FOR COACHES AND
TEACHERS. Dubuque, Iowa: William C. Brown Publishers, 1971. 162 p.

As the title indicates this book is designed for teachers and coaches.
Volleyball skills are analyzed in detail and offensive and defensive
strategies are thoroughly explained. Suggestions for training, conditioning, and prevention of injury are provided. The chapter on

coaching for effective performance is primarily an overview of factors affecting learning with suggestions for application to volley-ball coaching. A final chapter outlines administrative procedures for conducting a volleyball program.

Thigpen, Janet. POWER VOLLEYBALL FOR GIRLS AND WOMEN. 2d ed. Dubuque, Iowa: William C. Brown Co., 1974. 144 p. Paperbound.

This instructional manual is a presentation of the sport of volley-ball as it applies to girls and women; however, much of the infor-mation would be applicable to any player. A brief history includ-ing volleyball organizations and the national and international scene introduces the book. Other chapters are devoted to analysis of offensive and defensive skills and strategies, teaching progres-sions, a "typical" coaching session, and the psychology of coach-ing. A final section lists results of major tournaments for both men and women.

MISCELLANEOUS

Abbinananti, D., et al. OFFICIATING WOMEN'S SPORTS. 2d ed. Cham-paign, Ill.: Stipes Publishing Co., 1977. 104 p. Paperbound.

Techniques for officiating basketball, field hockey, softball, and volleyball are included in this instructional manual. Responsibili-ties and skills for officials in each sport are described and illus-trated. Contrasts and similarities among the current governing bodies such as the National Association for Girls and Women in Sport and the Amateur Athletic Union are also clarified. The or-ganization of the book makes it an easy-to-use source for officiat-ing techniques.

Barrilleaux, Doris, and Murray, Jim. INSIDE WEIGHT TRAINING FOR WOMEN. Chicago: Contemporary Books, 1978. 69 p. Paperbound.

The differences between weight training and weight lifting are clarified in this book, and a basic exercise program using weights is presented for women. Techniques for general conditioning and exercises for special areas of the body are included. A final chapter discusses strength and the female athlete.

Charles, Allegra. HOW TO WIN AT LADIES DOUBLES. New York: Arco Publishing Co., 1975. 151 p. Paperbound.

The title of this book will be a bit misleading to readers who ex-pect a thorough analysis of the techniques of doubles strategy. In a series of numerous but very brief chapters, the author does out-line the basics of doubles play; however, woven in between such sections as "Proper Position" and "How to Get to the Net" are several chapters on basic fundamentals of tennis--grips, drives, the serve, the lob, etc. Following those she discusses such diverse topics as tennis rackets, court surfaces, tennis elbow, and tennis and sex.

Cooper, Gwen, and Haas, Evelyn. WADE A LITTLE DEEPER, DEAR. San Francisco: California Living Books, 1979. 107 p.

This book is a guide to fly-fishing written specifically for the female reader. Information is included on the basics of fishing etiquette, the use of wet and dry flies, how to tie knots, and easy recipes for cooking the "catch." The book is written in a simple straightforward manner, rather than in technical terms and is one of the very few in this subject area.

Gould, Shirley. SWIMMING THE SHANE GOULD WAY. New York: Sterling Publishing Co., 1972. 160 p.

This book written by Shane Gould's mother contains a wide range of information about swimming and the competitive swimmer. Chapters on the freestyle, breaststroke, butterfly, and backstroke analyze the strokes as they are performed by Shane. Training and conditioning techniques and the fine points of racing competition are provided in other sections. In a more personal vein the author explores other aspects of swimming competition: "The Triangle: Parents-Coach-Swimmer" and "Living with a Champion." Though not a coach herself, Mrs. Gould provides useful and detailed information for the training of a competitive female swimmer.

Haney, Lynn. RIDE 'EM COWGIRL! New York: G.P. Putnam's Sons, 1975. 128 p.

Utilizing an informal writing style and the colorful terminology of the rodeo, author Haney successfully conveys the atmosphere of the rodeo world in which women participate. She explains the structure of professional rodeo, including the seven events of all-girl rodeos under the aegis of the Girls' Rodeo Association, and the two events of the Rodeo Cowboys' Association which women may enter--barrel racing and team roping.

Hunt, Lesley. INSIDE TENNIS FOR WOMEN. Chicago: Contemporary Books, 1978. 126 p. Paperbound.

Hunt's instructional manual on tennis for women is an attempt to deal with the special attributes and demands of the game that are different from those of the men's game. Using a narrative style she analyzes the skills of the game in detail, then further clarifies the analysis with photographs, diagrams, and brief comments related to them. Strategy for both singles and doubles play is described, and a chapter on "The Mental Game" offers suggestions for developing concentration and handling "nerves" in competitive play. Basic information on scoring and court etiquette is also included. While

advanced players may find useful information in the book, it is
designed primarily for less experienced players.

Jensen, Marlene. IMPROVE YOUR FIGURE THROUGH SPORTS. Chatsworth,
Calif.: Books for Better Living, 1974. 166 p. Paperbound.

To avoid the boredom of exercise for achieving and maintaining
fitness, Jensen suggests the fun of sports. Using a "cookbook"
approach, she describes the simplest skills needed for participating
in thirteen sports ranging from ping-pong to hang gliding. The
beginner may be able to make a start in some sports, but additional information and/or instruction will be needed for an accomplished
performance. The author's primary purpose, however, seems to be
encouraging sports participation rather than creating a champion.

Josey, Martha, with Pattie, Jane. FUNDAMENTALS OF BARREL RACING.
Houston: Cordovan Corp., 1969. 89 p. Paperbound.

Written in language for the beginner this book offers, in detail,
the necessary information for learning the sport of barrel racing
which is performed only by women at the professional level and
primarily by women at the amateur level. Josey provides advice
for selecting the right barrel horse, equipment, and costume; conditioning, training, and seasoning (working in different arenas) the
horse; techniques for horse and rider; and riding in competition.
A list of "dos and don'ts" at the end of each chapter further clarifies information for the potential barrel racer.

Lardner, Rex. TACTICS IN WOMEN'S SINGLES, DOUBLES, AND MIXED
DOUBLES. Garden City, N.Y.: Doubleday, 1975.

This book is devoted primarily to simple strategies, both offense
and defense. A brief review of basic tennis strokes is also included, along with a list of definitions of tennis terms.

Mayo, Jane, with Gray, Bob. CHAMPIONSHIP BARREL RACING. 3d ed.
Houston: Cordovan Corp., 1975. 85 p. Paperbound.

In this book, purported to be the first written on barrel racing,
Mayo summarizes the history of the sport and describes the important aspects of selecting and training the barrel horse. In chapters
titled "Kindergarten," "Grade School," "High School," and "Grad-
uation," she provides a progressive analysis of the skills and techniques needed to become a successful barrel racer.

Sauser, Jean, and Shay, Arthur. INSIDE RACQUETBALL FOR WOMEN. Chicago: Contemporary Books, 1977. 107 p.

Believing that a different approach from that for men should be
taken in teaching racquetball to women, the authors have written
this book for the beginning woman player. The basic format is one

of presenting the common errors of the game in narrative and photographs along with corrections for the error on the adjoining page. In this manner both basic skills and game strategy are effectively covered. The authors conclude with a summary of rules and a glossary of racquetball terms.

Seghers, Carroll. THE PEAK EXPERIENCE: A GUIDE TO HIKING AND CLIMBING FOR WOMEN. Indianapolis: Bobbs-Merrill Co., 1979. 224 p.

The woman who is interested in participating in mountain hiking and climbing will find helpful information in this elementary guide. Topics such as preliminary training and planning are covered, but plans for setting up a Himalayan expedition may be out of place in a guide for beginners. Of particular interest is a chapter that attempts to dispel some of the myths about the effects of strenuous exercise on women's physiques.

Sloane, Gloria, and Coe, Phyllis. HOW TO BE A FIRST-RATE FIRST MATE: A SAILING GUIDE FOR WOMEN. New York: Quadrangle/The New York Times Book Co., 1974. 156 p.

This factual guide is primarily a check list of practical items for helping to make boating a happy experience. Such items as safety, planning cruises, equipping the galley, entertaining guests, sailing with children, rules of the "road," handling the boat on the water, and care of the boat on the return offer practical suggestions for the novice sailor. Some readers may be displeased with subtle nuances that infer a second-class position for the woman sailor.

Sperber, Paula, with Pezzano, Chuck. INSIDE BOWLING FOR WOMEN. Chicago: Contemporary Books, 1977. 74 p.

Professional bowler Sperber has used an informal style of writing to provide diverse information about the sport of bowling. In addition to advice about skill performance, she discusses such topics as appropriate dress, selecting equipment, conditioning exercises, league and tournament competition, and situations such as pregnancy that may make bowling different for women, at least for a time.

Part IV

PERIODICALS, FILMS, AND

OTHER SOURCES OF INFORMATION

As women's sports programs have developed and participation by women has increased, a growing acceptance of the athletic female has also occurred. Many sporting opportunities are currently available at all levels of participation for the interested woman. Concurrent with these developments has been increased recognition for the woman in sport. A number of conferences devoted to women and sport have explored the many aspects of such endeavors; films of women in sporting activities not only suggest that these are now appropriate female pursuits but also depict sportswomen as persons striving for excellence just as men are frequently depicted. Periodicals devoted entirely to women's sporting achievements and interests are now being published.

This section is an attempt to compile sources of information that generally have been unconcerned with women in sport until recently. The exception to this lack of concern is the sports organization. Many of the women's organizations have been in existence for a long time, and many of those with both men and women members have included women from the time of establishment. Chapter 8 lists women's sports periodicals currently available and other sport publications which may carry articles about women. Chapter 9 includes films about women in sport. Reports from conferences on women and sport are found in chapter 10, and sports halls of fame that include women among their honored members are listed in chapter 11. National organizations concerned with women's sports are found in chapter 12, as well as other sports organizations that include women in their membership or sponsor women's activities.

While sources for information about women in sport may appear limited, they are increasing rapidly. In time, perhaps the literature of women and sport will attain a level commensurate with the interest and achievements of sportswomen everywhere.

Chapter 8

PERIODICALS

WOMEN'S SPORTS MAGAZINES

COACHING: WOMEN'S ATHLETICS (formerly COACH: WOMEN'S ATHLE-
TICS and WOMAN COACH). Wallingford, Conn.: Intercommunications,
1975-- . Bimonthly, except July and August.

> The information presented in this magazine covers a broad range
> of topics. Coaching techniques for a wide variety of sports are
> included as well as training and conditioning information. A spe-
> cial features section is devoted to topics of general interest in the
> area of women's sports. Recent issues include department sections
> devoted to special information such as legal liability, athletics
> for women, the United States Olympic Committee, and sports medi-
> cine. An annual guide to schools offering athletic scholarships to
> women is provided. The magazine should be of particular interest
> to persons involved in women's athletic programs. Business ad-
> dress: Intercommunications, P.O. Box 867, 50 South Main Street,
> Wallingford, Conn. 06492.

INSIDE WOMEN'S TENNIS. San Mateo, Calif.: Program Publications, 1977--
Biweekly.

> This brief tabloid is devoted entirely to women's tennis and in-
> cludes articles about both amateur and professional players and
> tournaments. Business office: Program Publications, 1660 South
> Amphlett Boulevard, Suite 266, San Mateo, Calif. 94402.

IN THE RUNNING. Washington, D.C.: SPRINT, 1978-- . Quarterly.

> This newsletter is a project of the Women's Equity Action League
> (WEAL) Educational and Legal Defense Fund. The information is
> devoted entirely to women's sports and particular emphasis is placed
> on information about sex equity in sports. Business office: SPRINT,
> 805 Fifteenth Street, N.W., Washington, D.C. 20005.

THE LADY GOLFER. Scottsdale, Ariz.: Seidal Publications, 1968-- . Ten
issues annually.

This magazine provides a record of most organized golf activities in the United States and the winners of major tournaments throughout the country. Feature stories usually focus on individual women golfers, and articles on golf instruction appear regularly. Continuing departments are "Know Your Rules," "Scoreboard," and "Tournament Dates." Business address: Seidal Publications, Box 1118, Scottsdale, Ariz. 85252.

MADEMOISELLE GYMNAST. Vols. 1-5. Santa Monica: Sundby Publications, 1966-71. Bimonthly, except July and August.

This publication was devoted entirely to women's gymnastics. Instructional techniques were often presented, and the accomplishments of world-class gymnasts and potential champions were regularly reported. Major gymnastic events for women around the world were covered, and continuing features included a book review section and names in the news. MADEMOISELLE GYMNAST was absorbed by GYMNAST in 1972 (later changed to INTERNATIONAL GYMNAST), and that magazine carries information about both women's and men's gymnastics. Business office: Sundby Publications, 410 Broadway, Santa Monica, Calif. 90401.

SOUTHERN CALIFORNIA GIRLS SPORTS. Santa Maria, Calif.: Southern California Girls Sports, 1978-- . Monthly, except August and September.

A tabloid-type newspaper, this monthly periodical deals primarily with women's sports activities in southern California. It does, however, include a variety of topics from reports of sports personalities to activities on the collegiate scene. The format and focus on women's sport involvement might well serve as a model for other locales. Business office: 301 East Chapel, Suite 204, Santa Maria, Calif. 93454.

THE SPORTSWOMAN. Lafayette, Calif.: Sportswoman, 1973-- . Monthly, irregular in recent years.

This magazine carries articles in each issue on a variety of sports for women. These range from instructional tips in many of the common sports to reports of the more unusual activities in which women participate, such as minibike racing, jousting, and aerobatics. Regular features include "Coaches' Corner," "Sportswomen in the News," "Readers' Forum," and "News and Comments." The magazine regularly provides information about women's collegiate events. Business office: Sportswoman, 3732 Mt. Diablo Boulevard, Lafayette, Calif. 94549.

UNITED STATES WOMEN COACHES AND ATHLETES. Brooklyn: Five Women Publishing Co., 1978-- . Monthly, except July and August.

This magazine focuses on women's athletics and includes instructional information as well as articles on individual athletes and athletic teams. Continuing features include a monthly sports calendar; super stars, which highlights accomplishments of selected women athletes; a new products section; and a sports quiz section. Activities in almost all sports areas in which women participate are covered. Business Office: Five Women Publishing Co., 1713 Sheepshead Bay Road, Brooklyn, N.Y. 11235.

THE WOMAN BOWLER. Greendale, Wis.: Women's International Bowling Congress, 1936-- . Monthly, except bimonthly, May-August.

Information concerning the entire spectrum of women's bowling is covered in this periodical. Continuing features are National Leaders, All-Americans Speak, Bowling Better, National 600 Bowling Club, and Memo from WIBC. Articles of general bowling interest appear regularly. Business address: WIBC, 5301 South 76th Street, Greendale, Wis. 53129.

WOMAN GOLFER. Encino, Calif.: Daisy Publishing Co., 1977-- . Bimonthly.

This magazine deals with women's golf, both amateur and professional. Articles range from instructional techniques and equipment information to features on individual players. Continuing departments are amateur and LPGA results, a golf fashions section, book reviews, and nostalgia, a historical section. Business address: Daisy Publishing Co., 16200 Ventura Boulevard, Encino, Calif. 91436.

WOMEN'S COACHING CLINIC. Englewood Cliffs, N.J.: Prentice-Hall, 1977-- . Monthly.

This magazine is devoted entirely to information on coaching women's sports. A variety of activities is covered, and material ranges from techniques of skill and strategy to the psychological aspects of coaching. Business address: Prentice-Hall, Englewood Cliffs, N.J. 07632.

WOMENSPORTS. Vols. 1-5. New York: Charter Publishing Co., 1974-78. Monthly.

Published by Billie Jean King until it ceased publication with the February, 1978 issue, WOMENSPORTS was devoted to information about women and sport. Regular features included a calendar of women's sports events; a section on "new faces" on the sports scene; scoreboard, which noted winners in major events; and usually a section on "foremothers," early sports heroines. Information covered a wide variety of topics, both the usual sports in which women participate as well as the unusual. Business office: Charter Publishing Co., 230 Park Avenue, New York, N.Y. 10017.

WOMEN'S SPORTS. Palo Alto, Calif.: Women's Sports Publication, 1979-- . Monthly.

With the demise of WOMENSPORTS in 1978, this new publication, included with membership in the Women's Sports Foundation, seems destined to replace the earlier periodical devoted to women's sports. The magazine regularly includes information from the foundation; a calendar of women's sports events; a record column of people and their performances; and a column on health, nutrition, and beauty for the athlete. Future issues are to include a monthly commentary about women's sports from a prominent figure in such fields as government, politics, art, or literature as well as articles of general sports interest. Business address: Women's Sports Magazine, P.O. Box 50483, Palo Alto, Calif. 94303.

PERIODICALS WITH REGULAR OR OCCASIONAL ARTICLES ON WOMEN'S SPORTS

AAU NEWS. 3400 West 86th Street, Indianapolis, Ind. 46268. 1930-- . Monthly.

AMERICAN FENCING. Amateur Fencers League of America, 601 Curtis Street, Albany, Calif. 94706. 1949-- . Bimonthly.

ATHLETIC JOURNAL. Athletic Journal Publishing Co., 1719 Howard Street, Evanston, Ill. 60202. 1921-- . Monthly, except July and August.

ATHLETIC TRAINING. National Athletic Trainers Association, Eastern Associates, P.O. Box 1865, Greenville, N.C. 27834. 1972-- . Quarterly.

BADMINTON USA. United States Badminton Association, P.O. Box 237, Swartz Creek, Mich. 48473. 1937-- . Quarterly.

BICYCLING. Bicycling Magazine, 33 East Minor Street, Emmaus, Pa. 18049. 1960-- . Monthly, except bimonthly, September-February.

BIKE WORLD. World Publications, 1400 Stierlin Road, Mountain View, Calif. 94043. 1972-- . Bimonthly.

COLLEGE AND JUNIOR TENNIS. Junior Tennis, 100 Harbor Road, Port Washington, N.Y. 11050. 1971-- . Monthly.

GOLF DIGEST. Golf Digest, 297 Westport Avenue, Norwalk, Conn. 06856. 1950-- . Monthly.

GOLF GUIDE. Werner Book Corp., 631 Wilshire Boulevard, Santa Monica, Calif. 90401. 1974-- . Monthly.

GOLF ILLUSTRATED. Rich Publishers, Temecula, Calif. 92390. 1973-- . Quarterly.

GOLF MAGAZINE. 235 East 45th Street, New York, N.Y. 10017. 1959-- . Monthly.

GOLF WORLD. P.O. Box 2000, Southern Pines, N.C. 28387. 1947-- . Weekly.

GYMNASTICS WORLD. Sundby Sports, 410 Broadway, Santa Monica, Calif. 90401. 1974-- . Bimonthly.

JOURNAL OF SPORTS MEDICINE. Sports and Medicine Publishers, Brookfield Center, Conn. 06805. 1972-- . Bimonthly.

MEDICINE AND SCIENCE IN SPORTS. American College of Sports Medicine, 1440 Monroe Street, Madison, Wis. 53706. 1969-- . Quarterly.

OFFICIAL AMERICAN HORSEMAN. Stories, Layouts, and Press, 257 Park Avenue South, New York, N.Y. 10010. 1979-- . Monthly.

ON THE RUN. World Publication, 1400 Stierlin, Mountain View, Calif. 94043. 1978-- . Bimonthly.

THE PHYSICIAN AND SPORTS MEDICINE. McGraw-Hill, 4530 West 77th Street, Minneapolis, Minn. 55435. 1973-- . Monthly.

POPULAR BOWLING. Joan Publishing Co., Dunellen, N.J. 08812. 1960-- . Bimonthly.

PREP PIN PATTER. 1913 West 103d Street, Chicago, Ill. 60643. Monthly.

PROFESSIONAL GOLFERS ASSOCIATION OF AMERICA (formerly THE PROFESSIONAL GOLFER). PGA National Headquarters, P.O. Box 12458, Lake Park, Fla. 33403. 1920-- . Monthly.

RACQUET. Reflex Sports, 342 Madison Avenue, New York, N.Y. 10017. 1976-- . Bimonthly.

THE RUNNER. New York Times Communications Corp., One Park Avenue, New York, N.Y. 10016. 1978-- . Monthly.

RUNNER'S WORLD. World Publications, 1400 Stierlin, Mountain View, Calif. 94043. 1966-- . Monthly.

Periodicals

SCHOLASTIC COACH. Scholastic Magazines, 50 West 44th Street, New York, N.Y. 10036. 1940-- . Monthly, except June, July, and August.

SKIING. Ziff-Davis Publishing Co., One Park Avenue, New York, N.Y. 10016. 1949-- . Seven times a year, September through spring.

SKI MAGAZINE. United States Ski Association, 1726 Champa Street, Suite 300, Denver, Colo. 80202. 1948-- . Monthly.

SOCCER AMERICA. 833 1/2 Bancroft Avenue, Berkeley, Calif. 94623. 1964-- . Weekly.

SOCCER CORNER. Daisy Publishing Co., 16200 Ventura Boulevard, Encino, Calif. 91436. 1977-- . Monthly except November-February.

SOCCER DIGEST. 1020 Church Street, Evanston, Ill. 60201. 1978-- . Monthly.

SOCCER MONTHLY. Spencer Marketing Services, 370 Lexington Avenue, New York, N.Y. 10017. 1974-- . Monthly, except bimonthly, July and August.

SOCCER NEWS. Soccer Publications, Box 153, New Rochelle, N.Y. 10802. 1943-78. Monthly.

SOCCER WORLD. World Publications, 1400 Stierlin, Mountain View, Calif. 94043. 1974-- . Bimonthly.

SPORT. MVP Sports, 641 Lexington Avenue, New York, N.Y. 10022. 1946-- . Monthly.

SPORTSCOPE. P.O. Box 1829, Denver, Colo. 80201. 1972-- . Weekly.

SPORTS ILLUSTRATED. Time, 541 North Fairbanks Court, Chicago, Ill. 60611. 1954-- . Weekly.

SWIMMING WORLD AND JUNIOR SWIMMER. Swimming World, P.O. Box 45497, Los Angeles, Calif. 90045. 1960-- . Monthly.

TEE IT UP. National Junior Golfers Association, P.O. Box 27538, Station 7, Atlanta, Ga. 30327.

TENNIS. Tennis Features, 495 Westport Avenue, Norwalk, Conn. 06856. 1965-- . Monthly.

TENNIS, MAGAZINE OF THE RACQUET SPORTS. 495 Westport, Norwalk, Conn. 06856. 1965-- . Monthly.

TENNIS ILLUSTRATED. 630 Shatto Place, Los Angeles, Calif. 90005. 1974-- . Monthly.

TENNIS TRADE. Hoffman Press, 3000 France Avenue, South, Minneapolis, Minn. 55416. 1972-- . Monthly.

TENNIS USA. Chilton Co., Chilton Way, Radnor, Pa. 19089. 1938-- . Monthly.

TRACK AND FIELD NEWS. Box 296, Los Altos, Calif. 94022. 1948-- . Monthly.

USA VOLLEYBALL REVIEW. United States Volleyball Association, 1750 East Boulder Street, Boulder, Colo. 80909. 1975-- . Bimonthly.

VOLLEYBALL MAGAZINE. 9420-D Activity Road, San Diego, Calif. 92126. Bimonthly.

WORLD TENNIS. CBS Publications, 1515 Broadway, New York, N.Y. 10036. 1953-- . Monthly.

YOUNG ATHLETE. P.O. Box 246, Mount Morris, Ill. 61054. 1975-- . Bimonthly.

YOUTH SOCCER MAGAZINE. Matson Publishing Co., 3715 West Lomita Boulevard, Suite 115, Torrance, Calif. 90505. 1978-- . Monthly.

Chapter 9

FILMS

MOTION PICTURES

COLGATE WOMEN'S SPORTS SPECIAL. ABC Sports, 1974. Motion picture. 16mm, 56 min., sound, color.

> The talents and achievements of several outstanding women in sports are discussed in this film. Dinah Shore hosts the film which features sportswomen Billie Jean King, Olga Korbut, Princess Anne, and Susie Berning.

THE FLASHETTES. New Day Films, 1977. Motion picture. 16mm, 20 min., sound, color.

> This is a documentary film about a black, all girls' track team from Bedford-Stuyvescent in Brooklyn. The activities of the girls and their growing self-confidence as a result of team membership are portrayed in the film.

THE FLOW OF MOVEMENT IN RHYTHMICAL GYMNASTICS. University of Iowa, 1968. Motion picture. 16mm, 20 min., sound, color.

> This film explores the meaning of rhythmical gymnastics in group performance and individual movements. A few basic exercises stressing the importance of natural harmonious movements involving the total body are introduced, and routines are presented by the Finnish gymnasts of the University of Helsinki.

FOR THE LOVE OF A HORSE. Film Arts, 1973. Motion Picture. 16mm, 14 min., sound, color.

> The joys of a young girl learning to ride horses is depicted in this film.

GIRLS SPORTS: ON THE RIGHT TRACK. Cine Design Associates, 1976. Motion picture. 16mm, 17 min., sound, color.

> The limited opportunities available for women to compete in sport-

ing events are considered in this film. An attempt is made to show how these limitations are being replaced by new opportunities for women in a variety of competitive sports, including track and field.

JOAN WESTON. Oxford Films, 1973. Motion picture. 16mm, 22 min., sound, color.

Roller skater Joan Weston is featured in this film which provides a behind-the-scenes look at the world of the roller derby.

JO JO STARBUCK AND KEN SHELLEY. Cine Design Associates, 1972. Motion picture. 16mm, 12 min., sound, color.

Ice skaters Jo Jo Starbuck and Ken Shelley, who turned professional, are shown performing in this film as amateurs in national and international competition.

KIKI CUTTER BEATTIE. Oxford Films, 1973. Motion picture. 16mm, 22 min., sound, color.

Kiki Cutter Beattie, former amateur skiing champion, is featured in this film as she competes for top prize money in the first professional ski race for women.

LOOK AT LADY NOW. Cine Design Associates, 1976. Motion picture. 16mm, 51 min., sound, color.

Hosted by former gymnastic champion Cathy Rigby, this film presents a history of women's involvement in sports from the early 1900s to the present time.

1972 WOMEN'S OLYMPIC TRACK AND FIELD INSTRUCTIONAL FILM. Track and Field News, 1973. Motion picture. 16mm, 20 min., silent, black and white.

The women athletes who competed in the track and field events in the 1972 Olympics in Munich are featured in this film. Captions are included on the silent film.

1976 KODAK WOMEN'S ALL-AMERICAN BASKETBALL TEAM. Eastman Kodak Co., 1977. Motion picture. 16mm, 20 min., sound, color.

This film features the ten outstanding college women basketball players who are selected each year by the Women's National Basketball Coaching Clinic.

OLGA: A FILM PORTRAIT. Carousel Films, 1975. Motion picture. 16mm, 47 min., sound, color.

This film presents a biographical study of Russian gymnast Olga

Korbut. The picture exemplifies the special athletic training received by Russian athletes, the personal determination needed to reach perfection, and the effort necessary to remain the best.

SWEETHEART OF THE RODEO. British Columbia Department of Agriculture, 1975. Motion picture. 16mm, 24 min., sound, color.

The rodeo success of Dee Watt, the British Columbia champion of barrel racing, is featured in this film.

VOLLEYBALL--DIG IT. BFA Educational Media, 1974. Motion picture. 16mm, 13 min., sound, color.

Volleyball expert Kathy Gregory discusses the skills of playing volleyball in this film. Demonstrations of skills and techniques of play are presented by several outstanding women players.

WHAT MAKES SALLY RUN? King Broadcasting Co., 1974. Motion picture. 16mm, 25 min., sound, color.

The prejudice and lack of backing which women's athletics have suffered in the United States is recounted in this film, which also presents national and world-class women athletes in the Puget Sound area.

WHO'S ON FIRST--A STORY OF GIRLS' SPORTS. JAB Film Library, 1975. Motion picture. 16mm, 13 min., sound, color.

This film examines the stereotype of girls in sports by following the members of a winning junior high school girls' softball team as they prepare for and play their most difficult game of the season.

WOMEN AND SPORTS: BASKETBALL. Coca-Cola Co., 1976. Motion Picture. 16mm, 11 min., sound, color.

This film is the first in a series of motivational films about girls' and women's sports. It is directed primarily at junior high and high school athletes; however, it may also be useful for college students.

WOMEN AND SPORTS: GYMNASTICS. Coca-Cola Co., 1977. Motion Picture. 16mm, 15 min., sound, color.

The 1977 collegiate women's gymnastics competition is presented in this film, which also includes comments from coaches, gymnastics training sessions, and slow-motion segments of performances.

WOMEN AND SPORTS: VOLLEYBALL. Coca-Cola Co., 1977. Motion Picture. 16mm, 13 min., sound, color.

This film highlights the thrill and excitement of the increasingly popular sport of volleyball. Segments of play are presented from the 1977 National Invitational Women's Volleyball Tournament held at the University of California, Los Angeles.

WOMEN GOLD MEDALISTS. CTV Television Network, 1976. Motion Picture. 16mm, 50 min., sound, color.

This film is a television special from the CTV program, Olympiad. Women athletes from various Olympic competitions are honored for their winning performances.

WOMEN IN SPORTS. Cine Design Associates, 1976. Motion Picture. 16mm, 28 min., sound, color.

Woman's participation in sports is surveyed from classical times to the present day. The film discusses prejudices against the physically active woman, the growing awareness of women's rights as sports participants, and the new enthusiasm of women for sports.

WOMEN'S BASKETBALL--JUMP BALL. BFA Educational Media, 1976. Motion Picture. 16mm, 15 min., sound, color.

This film attempts to provide incentive and motivation for women to play and enjoy basketball. The importance of practice and determination in developing the basic skills of the game is stressed as well as how togetherness between teammates and coach can make the difference in winning and losing.

WOMEN'S TRACK AND FIELD. Mankato State University Memorial Library, 1976. Loop films. Super 8mm, 8 min., silent, color.

Women's track and field events from the 1976 Montreal Olympic Games are presented in this film. Included are the 100-, 200-, and 1500-meter runs; the 100-meter hurdles; the 4 X 100-meter relay; the long jump, high jump, and discus throw.

YOUNG AND JUST BEGINNING. National Film Board of Canada, 1975. Motion Picture. 16mm, 29 min., sound, color.

The work of a ten-year-old gymnast is featured in this film. Her present training and her prospects as a 1980 Olympics contender are reviewed.

YOUNG WOMEN IN SPORTS. BFA Educational Media, 1974. Motion Picture. 16mm, 16 min., sound, color.

Through personal interviews this film examines the attitudes of four young women athletes about strength, competition, and themselves as women and as athletes.

YOUR MOVE. Films Incorporated, 1970. Motion picture. 16mm, 22 min., sound, color.

> The myths and taboos which have prevented women from participating in and enjoying competitive and recreational sports are presented. A variety of sports activities are shown, and the film encourages girls and women to participate and to enjoy physical activity.

PRODUCERS AND DISTRIBUTORS

ABC SPORTS. 1330 Avenue of the Americas, New York, N.Y. 10019.

BFA EDUCATIONAL MEDIA. 2211 Michigan Avenue, Santa Monica, Calif. 90404.

BRITISH COLUMBIA DEPARTMENT OF AGRICULTURE. Information Branch, Victoria, B.C., Canada.

CAROUSEL FILMS, INCORPORATED. 1501 Broadway, Suite 1503, New York, N.Y. 10036.

CINE DESIGN ASSOCIATES. P.O. Box 5905, Pasadena, Calif. 91107.

COCA-COLA COMPANY. P.O. Drawer 1743, Atlanta, Ga. 30302.

EASTMAN KODAK CO. Audio Visual Library Distribution, 343 State Street, Rochester, N.Y. 14650.

FILM ARTS, LIMITED. 161 Church Street, Toronto, Ontario, Canada.

FILMS, INCORPORATED. 1144 Wilmette Avenue, Wilmette, Ill. 60091.

JAB FILM LIBRARY. P.O. Box 213, Fair Lawn, N.J. 07410.

KING BROADCASTING CO. 320 Aurora Avenue, North, Seattle, Wash. 98109.

NATIONAL FILM BOARD OF CANADA. 1251 Avenue of the Americas, New York, N.Y. 10020.

NEW DAY FILMS. 779 Susquehanna Avenue, Franklin Lakes, N.J. 07417.

OXFORD FILMS. 1136 North Las Palmas Avenue, Hollywood, Calif. 90038.

TRACK AND FIELD NEWS. P.O. Box 296, Los Altos, Calif. 94022.

UNIVERSITY OF IOWA. Motion Picture Unit, Audio Visual Center, Iowa City, Iowa. 52240.

Chapter 10
CONFERENCE REPORTS

THE COLGATE WOMEN'S SPORTS MEDICINE SYMPOSIUM. New York: Colgate Sports Medicine Corporate Communications, 1978. 24 p. Paperbound.

Papers on training, nutrition, muscle testing, positive habits for athletes, proper running shoes, and exploding the myths about female athletes were presented at the first Colgate Women's Sports Medicine Symposium. This booklet includes by-lined material excerpted from those presentations. Although the selected material is brief, it provides a substantial amount of information for each of the topics.

CONFERENCE ON WOMEN, SPORTS AND THE LAW. Los Angeles: University of Southern California, 1976. 691 p.

The written materials available from this conference are not reports of the speakers' addresses, but consist of a 691-page book of cases, statutes, regulations, and articles concerning the legal aspects of sex discrimination in the area of athletics. The five sections of the book are devoted to "An Overview," "Equal Rights for Women in Athletic Programs Conducted Outside of Schools and Colleges," "School Athletic Conference and Association Rules and Equal Protection Requirements," "Title IX of the Education Amendments of 1972," and the "NCAA and Women's Sports." The report is available from the Advanced Professional Program, University of Southern California Law Center, University Park, Los Angeles, Calif. 90007.

Eastern Association of Physical Education for College Women. PROCEEDINGS OF THE ANNUAL FALL CONFERENCE: THE CHANGING SCENE. Chicopee, Mass.: 1974. 73 p. Paperbound.

This report is a compilation of presentations given at the Annual Conference of Eastern Association of Physical Education for College Women which focused on the central theme of women in sport and athletics. Major addresses were made by Celeste Ulrich, Margaret Dunkle, Katherine Ley, and Ann Jewett, and all dealt essentially with the changing role of woman in sport.

Conference Reports

Harris, Dorothy V., ed. WOMEN AND SPORT: A NATIONAL RESEARCH CONFERENCE. Penn State HPER Series, no. 2. University Park: Pennsylvania State University, 1972. 416 p. Paperbound.

> This report presents the papers from a conference, August 13-18, 1972, whose central focus was the female's involvement in physical activity and sport. The conference was organized around topics related to the psychological, sociological, physiological, and biomechanical aspects of the female in sport, and the papers of the twenty-two speakers are presented in their entirety. Only one paper is found in the biomechanical area and four in the physiological; thus, the proceedings may be of more value to persons interested in the psychological or sociological areas, which include eleven and seven papers, respectively.

NATIONAL CONFERENCE ON SPORTS PROGRAMS FOR COLLEGE WOMEN. Washington, D.C.: American Association for Health, Physical Education, and Recreation, 1970. 73 p. Paperbound.

> This report presents the major addresses from the 1969 women's sports conference in Denver, Colorado, sponsored by the Division for Girls' and Women's Sports. The purpose of the conference was to examine the present status and future directions of sports for college women, and presentations focused on those areas. The conference report is limited, however, because of space allowances for speeches which resulted in either revised or abridged texts from the speakers.

NATIONAL CONFERENCE ON WOMEN AND SPORT. Ottawa, Ontario: Health and Welfare Canada, 1974. 80 p. Paperbound.

> Summaries of the major addresses and workshop presentations given at the first National Conference on Women and Sport in Toronto in May, 1974 are included in this conference report. Imperatives for change, action proposals, and strategies for change as these relate to women and sport are also presented. Although major points made by speakers are included, the value of the report may be lessened because of the summarizing for publication.

Pearson, Kathleen, et al., eds. WOMEN AND SPORTS: CONFERENCE PROCEEDINGS. Macomb: Western Illinois University, 1973. 197 p. Paperbound.

> The fifteen major addresses of this conference on Women and Sports are presented in their entirety in this report. A different discipline was examined on each of the five days of the conference under the topics of history, philosophy, social psychology, administration, and physiological and biomechanical considerations. Almost all of the papers include many bibliographical references related to the topic.

WOMEN IN SPORTS: BRUDER CONFERENCE. Immaculata, Pa.: Immaculata
College, 1975. 61 p. Paperbound.

The presentations of eleven speakers at the Bruder Conference on
Women in Sports, December 4, 1975 are included in this confer-
ence proceedings. Papers were presented by Joe Paterno, Thomas
Boslooper, Barbara Lockhart, Cathy Rush, Helen Harris Solomons,
Nicholas John Robak, Russell L. Sturzebecker, Carole A. Ogles-
by, Dorothy V. Harris, Mary Jo Hoverbeck, and Jan Felshin.
Diverse subject matter ranged from the historical and physiological
aspects of sports for women to subjects such as contact sports for
women, media coverage of women in sports, and implications of
Title IX.

Chapter 11
SPORTS HALLS OF FAME

NATIONAL HALLS OF FAME

AMATEUR TRAPSHOOTING ASSOCIATION HALL OF FAME. Vandalia, Ohio 45377.

Eight women have been installed in this hall of fame, and biographical information is available for each of them. Candidates are selected from two groups: persons who have contributed to the growth of trapshooting and to the betterment of the sport, and shooters who have made impressive records in trapshooting. Candidates are eligible after twenty years of participation in the sport. The hall is open throughout the year.

AMERICAN BICYCLE HALL OF FAME. 260 West 260th Street, New York, N.Y. 10471.

Some biographical information is available at this hall of fame for the few women who are listed on the honor roll of members.

AQUATIC HALL OF FAME AND MUSEUM OF CANADA. 25 Poseidon Bay, Winnipeg, Manitoba, Canada R3M 3E4.

Women are included in this hall of fame which honors persons who have excelled in swimming, diving, water polo and synchronized swimming. An aquatics library is maintained by the hall, and it has an ancient history of aquatics which is particularly well depicted. The hall is open year-round.

BRITISH COLUMBIA SPORTS HALL OF FAME. P.O. Box 69020, Station K, Vancouver, B.C., Canada V5K 4A9.

Athletes who have reached a special excellent on a national or international level in sixty-eight different sports are eligible for membership in this hall. Some biographical information is available for members, many of whom are women. Scrapbooks, photographs, medals, trophies, mementos, and newspaper clippings provide additional information about athletes, coaches, and adminis-

trators who have been selected for membership. The hall is open
year-round except holidays.

CANADA'S SPORTS HALL OF FAME. Exhibition Place, Toronto, Ontario,
Canada M6K 3C3.

This hall of fame recognizes individuals who have attained success
in a variety of sports activities. The thirty-two women who have
been honored with membership represent such sports as archery,
figure skating, swimming, synchronized swimming, skiing, track,
golf, and trapshooting. Biographical information for each member
is available from the hall, which is open year-round.

CIRCUS HALL OF FAME. P.O. Drawer AH, Sarasota, Fla. 33578.

The Circus Hall of Fame was established to publicly honor circus
stars; collect and display mementos of the stars; maintain a circus
historical library; develop and train stars of the future; and create
a true understanding of the circus. Several women are hall of
fame members, and biographical information has been collected
for each of them. Activities such as acrobatics, equestrianship,
high wire, and lion tamer are represented among the women members. The hall is open year-round.

CITIZENS SAVINGS ATHLETIC FOUNDATION (formerly HELMS ATHLETIC
FOUNDATION). 9800 South Sepulveda Boulevard, Los Angeles, Calif. 90045.

This foundation houses thirty-one separate sports halls of fame.
The majority of women members are found in the golf, tennis,
swimming-diving, synchronized swimming, and track and field
halls of fame, and in the women's basketball hall of fame. Some
biographical information is available for members. The foundation
also selects two "Athletes of the Year," one from southern and one
from northern California. In the years 1900 to 1977 nineteen women
were selected for this honor. World Trophy Awards are presented
to athletes on each continent, and fourteen North American women,
all from the United States, have been honored in the years from
1896-1975. A library for all sports is maintained, and the hall
is open year-round.

INTERNATIONAL SWIMMING HALL OF FAME, INC. 1 Hall of Fame Drive,
Fort Lauderdale, Fla. 33316.

Many of the approximately 200 members of this hall are women
recognized for their success as swimmers, divers, coaches, or
contributors to the sport. Each member has a display with photographs and memorabilia, and a biography has been compiled for
each. A library containing books, films, rare books, and a special reference section for research is maintained with the hall
which is open year-round.

INTERNATIONAL TENNIS HALL OF FAME. 194 Bellevue Avenue, Newport, R.I. 02840.

This hall of fame recognizes outstanding tennis players, and 30 of the 102 members are women. Biographical information is available for each member. The Tennis Museum, affiliated with the hall of fame, has a special display of one hundred years of women's tennis fashions. The hall of fame and museum are open year-round.

LADIES PROFESSIONAL GOLF HALL OF FAME. Augusta Golf and Country Club, Augusta, Ga. 30903.

Though not technically considered a national hall of fame, this hall does have members from throughout the United States. It is a project of the Ladies Professional Golf Association and maintains biographical information for members inducted into the hall.

NAISMITH MEMORIAL BASKETBALL HALL OF FAME. Alden Street, Box 175, Highland Station, Springfield, Mass. 01109.

Only a few women have currently been elected to the Basketball Hall of Fame. Biographical information and photographs are available for members. A library, archives, and museum are maintained in conjunction with the hall, which is open year-round except Thanksgiving, Christmas, and New Year's Day.

NATIONAL COWBOY HALL OF FAME AND HERITAGE CENTER. 1700 N.E. 63d Street, Oklahoma City, Okla. 73111.

A few women, particularly very early rodeo participants, have been inducted into this hall of fame. Biographical information and photographs are available for those members. The hall is open year-round except Thanksgiving, Christmas, and New Year's Day.

NATIONAL SKI HALL OF FAME. National Headquarters Division, P.O. Box 191, Ishpeming, Mich. 49849.

This hall of fame is owned and operated by the United States Ski Educational Foundation. The thirty-five members, about 16 percent are women, have all been ski athletes. The hall maintains a folder for each athlete which contains biographical information, photographs, and, in some cases, personal correspondence with the member. The hall is open year-round except Monday and Tuesday from September to June.

NATIONAL SOFTBALL HALL OF FAME. 2801 Northeast 50th Street, P.O. Box 11437, Oklahoma City, Okla. 73111.

The purpose of this hall of fame is to honor and give recognition to women and men who have distinguished themselves in amateur softball and have contributed to the growth and development of the sport. Twenty women, of the total of fifty-five in 1976, have been elected to the hall, including two of the first four members. Both slow-pitch and fast-pitch players are eligible. Biographical data and photographs are available for members. The hall and museum associated with it are open year-round.

NATIONAL TRACK AND FIELD HALL OF FAME. 1524 Kanawha Boulevard East, Charleston, W.Va. 25311.

The hall of fame encompasses all aspects of track and field and has inducted several women members since its founding in 1974. Biographical information and photographs are available for members who are chosen by a selection committee. Individuals are selected for their outstanding achievements in track and field as athletes, coaches, or contributors, but anyone may nominate persons for consideration to the selection committee. The hall maintains a library and is open year-round.

SAN DIEGO HALL OF CHAMPIONS. 1439 El Prado, Balboa Park, San Diego, Calif. 92101.

Founded to foster educational work particularly in the athletic and physical education realms, this hall gives recognition to athletes from the San Diego area who have won national and international acclaim. The hall recognizes stars of the month and stars of the year, many of whom are women. Some biographical data and photographs are available for each person elected to the hall of fame. The hall is open year-round, except Sundays.

WOMEN'S INTERNATIONAL BOWLING CONGRESS HALL OF FAME. 5301 South 76th Street, Greendale, Wis. 53129.

This hall shares facilities with the American Bowling Congress (for men) but is a separate entity. Members have been elected in three categories, Star of Yesteryear, recognizing past bowling achievement; Meritorious Service Award, honoring service, not necessarily bowling achievement or skill; and the Superior Performance Award, recognizing current significant individual bowling achievement. Some biographical data for members are available, and oil portraits of all inductees are displayed in the hall of fame at Bowling Headquarters. A bowling museum is maintained with the hall of fame, and both will be housed in a new building in a city other than Greendale in the near future.

WORLD GOLF HALL OF FAME. P.O. Box 908, Pinehurst, N.C. 28374.

Several women have been inducted into this hall of fame, which honors both amateur and professional players and persons who have supported the development of the game of golf. Biographical data and photographs are available for each member. Members are selected by the Golf Writers Association in three categories:

players up to 1930, modern players, and promoters of golf. The hall maintains a library and a collection of golfing artifacts and is open year-round except Christmas Day.

WOMEN'S STATE HALLS OF FAME

ARIZONA WOMEN'S BOWLING ASSOCIATION HALL OF FAME. Box 11436, Phoenix, Ariz. 85061.

CALIFORNIA WOMEN'S BOWLING HALL OF FAME. Box 3059, Bell Garden, Calif. 90201.

IOWA WOMEN'S BOWLING ASSOCIATION HALL OF FAME. 1615 Pierce, Sioux City, Iowa 51105.

MESA VALLEY WOMEN'S BOWLING ASSOCIATION HALL OF FAME. 1833 East Nielsen, Mesa, Ariz. 85204.

TEXAS WOMEN'S BOWLING ASSOCIATION HALL OF FAME. 117 Melbourne, Fort Worth, Tex. 76117.

WOMEN'S PROFESSIONAL BILLIARD ALLIANCE HALL OF FAME. 17 Strong Place, Brooklyn, N.Y. 11231.

Chapter 12

NATIONAL SPORTS ORGANIZATIONS

NATIONAL WOMEN'S SPORTS ORGANIZATIONS

ASSOCIATION FOR INTERCOLLEGIATE ATHLETICS FOR WOMEN. 1201 Sixteenth Street, N.W., Washington, D.C. 20036.

This association is the governing body for women's intercollegiate
athletics in the United States. Its purposes are to foster broad
programs of intercollegiate athletics for women; to assist member
schools to extend and enrich women's programs; to encourage excellence in performance of athletes; and to stimulate development
of quality leadership for women's programs. The association publishes an annual directory of members and a handbook and sponsors
twenty-one national championships for women.

CENTER FOR WOMEN AND SPORT. White Building, Pennsylvania State University, University Park, Pa. 16802.

The purpose of this center is to promote and conduct research on
the female in sport.

FEMINIST KARATE UNION. 101 Nickerson, Suite 250A, Seattle, Wash.
98109.

The purpose of this organization is to provide low-cost instruction
in self-defense and karate to women. Through workshops and
demonstrations, it attempts to educate the general public about
the problems of rape and assault on women and the importance
of self-defense.

GIRLS RODEO ASSOCIATION. 8909 Northeast 25th Street, Spencer, Okla.
73084.

This organization sponsors All-Girl Rodeos and conducts seminars
and clinics on the skills of horsemanship and rodeo events. Annual prize money for women rodeo champions is handled by this
association.

INTERNATIONAL SIDE-SADDLE ORGANIZATION. Box 2096, R.D. 2, Mount Holly, N.J. 08060.

> This organization promotes sidesaddle riding through clinics and all sidesaddle horse shows. SIDESADDLE NEWS is the monthly publication of the organization.

INTERNATIONAL WOMEN'S FISHING ASSOCIATION. P.O. Box 2025, Palm Beach, Fla. 33480.

> This association encourages fishing competition for women, sponsors fishing tournaments, and promotes conservation. It has also established a scholarship fund for graduate students in marine sciences. HOOKS AND LINES is the association's monthly publication.

LADIES PROFESSIONAL GOLF ASSOCIATION. 919 Third Avenue, New York, N.Y. 10022.

> This organization is composed of professional women golfers and educators. Records of tournaments, money winnings, and scoring are kept by the association, and it assists members in securing golf positions. It also maintains the Ladies Golf Hall of Fame in Augusta, Georgia.

MOTORMAIDS. 556 West Fourth Street, Chillicothe, Ohio 45601.

> This is an organization of women interested in motorcycling.

NATIONAL ASSOCIATION FOR GIRLS AND WOMEN IN SPORT. 1201 Sixteenth Street, N.W., Washington, D.C. 20036.

> This association is an affiliate of the American Alliance for Health, Physical Education, and Recreation, and its major purpose is to support and promote quality sports programs for girls and women. Substructures in the association such as the Affiliated Board of Officials, National Coaches Council, Athletic Training Council, and Organization of Athletic Administrators serve the special needs and interests of those areas. Official rule books for many women's sports are regularly published by the association.

NATIONAL INTERCOLLEGIATE WOMEN'S FENCING ASSOCIATION, 18 Pleasant Place, Kearny, N.J. 07032.

> This association is composed of colleges and universities with women's varsity fencing teams, and its major purpose is to promote fencing for women in collegiate institutions. It conducts fencing matches, workshops, and clinics and determines the members of the All-American Women's Fencing Team, selected annually.

NOW TASK FORCE ON WOMEN IN SPORTS. National NOW Action Center, 425 Thirteenth Street, N.W., Suite 1001, Washington, D.C. 20004.

This group is affiliated with the National Organization for Women. Its major function is working toward ending sex discrimination in physical education and athletic programs.

UNITED STATES FIELD HOCKEY ASSOCIATION. 4415 Buffalo Rd., North Chili, N.Y. 14514.

The purpose of this organization is to promote field hockey in the United States. It sponsors exhibition games, clinics, and an annual national tournament. The official publication is THE EAGLE, and the association also publishes official rules for the sport.

UNITED STATES WOMEN'S CURLING ASSOCIATION. 1201 Somerset Dr., Glenview, Ill. 60025.

This is an organization of amateur women curlers which sponsors the annual Women's National Bonspiel (curling tournament).

UNITED STATES WOMEN'S LACROSSE ASSOCIATION. R.D. 2, Boiling Springs, Pa. 17001.

Promotion of lacrosse for women is the major focus of this organization. It establishes rules for competition and sponsors a national tournament. CROSS-CHECKS is the official publication of the association.

UNITED STATES WOMEN'S SQUASH RACQUETS ASSOCIATION. Mustin Lane, Villanova, Pa. 19085.

The purpose of this association is to promote interest in the game of squash among women. It sponsors tournaments at all levels and conducts international competition with England and Australia.

UPPITY WOMEN (MOTORCYCLING). P.O. Box 81, Detroit, Mich. 48231.

This organization was established to set up a national directory of women motorcyclists; to put women cyclists in touch with each other; and to help women learn to ride and maintain their cycles.

WOMEN PROFESSIONAL BOWLERS ASSOCIATION. 205 West Wacker Drive, Suite 300, Chicago, Ill. 60606.

The purpose of this association is to promote bowling, to improve the status of its members to professional rank, and to promote relationships among bowlers, proprietors, and the press. It sponsors exhibition tournaments and compiles tournament statistics.

WOMEN'S EQUITY ACTION LEAGUE. 805 Fifteenth Street, N.W., Washington, D.C. 20005.

Although not an organization of members, SPRINT is a project of the Women's Equity Action League, which focuses on sports for

women. Its major purpose is to promote equal opportunity for
women in sports.

WOMEN'S INTERNATIONAL BOWLING CONGRESS. 5301 South 76th Street,
Greendale, Wis. 53129.

This organization is the sanctioning body for women's bowling in
the United States, Canada, Bermuda, and Puerto Rico. It provides
uniform qualifications, rules, and regulations governing sanctioned
teams, leagues, and tournaments, and sponsors annual championship tournaments. It publishes THE WOMAN BOWLER MAGAZINE
and maintains a hall of fame of women bowlers.

WOMEN'S MARTIAL ARTS UNION. P.O. Box 879, New York, N.Y. 10025.

This organization works toward increasing the interest of women
in the martial arts and developing self-defense skills for women
from the diverse techniques of the martial arts. Another objective
is to combat sexism in the martial arts clubs and tournaments.

WOMEN'S SPORTS FOUNDATION. 195 Moulton Street, San Francisco,
Calif. 94123.

This organization was established to encourage all women to become involved in sport for their own personal growth, to provide
new opportunities for women's sports development, and to keep
members informed of current sports activities. It also publicizes
women's sports through public-service advertising and local news-
letters. Members receive the foundation's monthly publication,
WOMEN'S SPORTS.

WOMEN'S TENNIS ASSOCIATION. 1604 Union Street, San Francisco, Calif.
94123.

This association was founded to provide professional women tennis
players with a unified voice and a means to negotiate for a better
living. It takes an active role in administering and promoting
the women's professional game worldwide. Members are professional players, and a special membership category is open to
women who earn a minimum of approximately $10,000 on the pro
circuit. The official publication of the association is INSIDE
WOMEN'S TENNIS.

NATIONAL SPORTS ORGANIZATIONS WITH
WOMEN'S MEMBERSHIP

AMATEUR ATHLETIC UNION OF THE UNITED STATES. 3400 West 86th Street,
Indianapolis, Ind. 46268.

AMATEUR FENCERS' LEAGUE OF AMERICA. 601 Curtis St., Albany, Calif. 94706.

AMATEUR SOFTBALL ASSOCIATION OF AMERICA. P.O. Box 11437, Oklahoma City, Okla. 73111.

AMATEUR TRAPSHOOTING ASSOCIATION. P.O. Box 246, West National Road, Vandalia, Ohio 45377.

AMERICAN ATHLETIC ASSOCIATION FOR THE DEAF. 3916 Lantern Avenue, Silver Springs, Md. 20902.

AMERICAN BLIND BOWLING ASSOCIATION. 150 North Bellaire Avenue, Louisville, Ky. 40206.

AMERICAN CANOE ASSOCIATION. P.O. Box 248, Lorton, Va. 22079.

AMERICAN CASTING ASSOCIATION. Picnic Hill, Jackson, Ky. 41339.

AMERICAN JUNIOR BOWLING CONGRESS. 5301 South 76th Street, Greendale, Wis. 53129.

AMERICAN MOTORCYCLIST ASSOCIATION. P.O. Box 141, Westerville, Ohio 43081.

AMERICAN PLATFORM TENNIS ASSOCIATION. Box 901, Upper Montclair, N.J. 07043.

AMERICAN SKI ASSOCIATION. 5830 S. Lake and Houston Parkway, Houston, Tex. 77049.

AMERICAN SKI TEACHERS ASSOCIATION OF NATUR TEKNIK. 321 Jefferson Ave., Westfield, N.J. 07090.

AMERICAN TURNERS. 415 E. Michigan St., Indianapolis, Ind. 46204.

AMERICAN WATER SKI ASSOCIATION. J.R. 520 and Carl Floyd Rd., Winter Haven, Fla. 33880.

APPALACHIAN MOUNTAIN CLUB. Five Joy Street, Boston, Mass. 02108.

BILLIARD CONGRESS OF AMERICA. 717 North Michigan Avenue, Chicago, Ill. 60611.

EASTERN TENNIS PATRONS. 22 East 49th Street, New York, N.Y. 10017.

INTER-COLLEGIATE YACHT RACING ASSOCIATION OF NORTH AMERICA. 8893 Melinda Court, Milan, Mich. 48160.

INTERNATIONAL AMATEUR SWIMMING FEDERATION. 2000 Financial Centre, Des Moines, Iowa 50309.

INTERNATIONAL COMMITTEE OF SPORTS FOR THE DEAF. Gallaudet College, Washington, D.C. 20002.

LEAGUE OF AMERICAN WHEELMEN. P.O. Box 988, Baltimore, Md. 21203.

LOS ANGELES AIKI KAI (AIKIDO). 8929 Ellis Avenue, Los Angeles, Calif. 90034.

NATIONAL ARCHERY ASSOCIATION OF THE UNITED STATES. 1951 Geraldson Drive, Lancaster, Pa. 17601.

NATIONAL DUCKPIN BOWLING CONGRESS. 711 14th Street, N.W., Washington, D.C. 20005.

NATIONAL FEDERATION OF STATE HIGH SCHOOL ASSOCIATIONS. 11724 Plaza Circle, P.O. Box 20626, Kansas City, Mo. 64195.

NATIONAL FIELD ARCHERY ASSOCIATION. Route Two, Box 514, Redlands, Calif. 92373.

NATIONAL HORSESHOE PITCHERS ASSOCIATION OF AMERICA. P.O. Box 1702, Auburn, Calif. 95603.

NATIONAL JUNIOR COLLEGE ATHLETIC ASSOCIATION. P.O. Box 1586, Hutchinson, Kans. 67501.

NATIONAL MUZZLE LOADING RIFLE ASSOCIATION. Friendship, Ind. 47021.

NATIONAL RIFLE ASSOCIATION OF AMERICA. 1600 Rhode Island, N.W., Washington, D.C. 20036.

NATIONAL SKEET SHOOTING ASSOCIATION. P.O. Box 28188, San Antonio, Tex. 78228.

NATIONAL WHEELCHAIR ATHLETIC ASSOCIATION. 40-24 62d Street, Woodside, N.Y. 11377.

PROFESSIONAL ARCHERS ASSOCIATION. 4711 S. Brennan Rd., Hemlock, Mich. 48626.

PROFESSIONAL SKI INSTRUCTORS OF AMERICA. 2015 S. Pontiac Way, Suite 1A, Denver, Colo. 80224.

ROAD RUNNERS CLUB OF AMERICA. 1226 Orchard Village, Manchester, Mo. 63011.

SOARING SOCIETY OF AMERICA. Box 66071, Los Angeles, Calif. 90066.

SPECIAL OLYMPICS. 1701 K Street, N.W., Suite 203, Washington, D.C. 20006.

TRACK AND FIELD ASSOCIATION OF THE UNITED STATES OF AMERICA. 10920 Ambassador Drive, Kansas City, Mo. 64153.

UNDERWATER SOCIETY OF AMERICA. 732 50th Street, West Palm Beach, Fla. 33407.

UNITED STATES BADMINTON ASSOCIATION. P.O. Box 237, Swartz Creek, Mich. 48473.

UNITED STATES DUFFERS ASSOCIATION. P.O. Box 283, Newport, Ky. 41072.

UNITED STATES FIGURE SKATING ASSOCIATION. City Hall Plaza, Boston, Mass. 02108.

UNITED STATES GOLF ASSOCIATION. Golf House, Far Hills, N.J. 07931.

UNITED STATES HANDBALL FEDERATION. 4101 Dempster Street, Skokie, Ill. 60076.

UNITED STATES JUDO FEDERATION. 21054 Sarah Hills Dr., Saratoga, Calif. 95070.

UNITED STATES PARACHUTE ASSOCIATION. 806 Fifteenth Street, N.W., Suite 444, Washington, D.C. 20005.

UNITED STATES POLO ASSOCIATION. Executive Plaza, Suite 706, Oak Brook, Ill. 60521.

UNITED STATES PROFESSIONAL TENNIS ASSOCIATION. 6701 Highway 58, Harrison, Tenn. 37341.

UNITED STATES RACQUETBALL ASSOCIATION. 4101 Dempster Street, Skokie, Ill. 60076.

UNITED STATES REVOLVER ASSOCIATION. 59 Alvin Street, Springfield, Mass. 01104.

UNITED STATES SKI ASSOCIATION. 1726 Champa Street, Suite 300, Denver, Colo. 80202.

UNITED STATES TABLE TENNIS ASSOCIATION. 1031 Jackson Street, St. Charles, Mo. 63301.

UNITED STATES TENNIS ASSOCIATION. 51 East 42d Street, New York, N.Y. 10017.

UNITED STATES TRACK AND FIELD FEDERATION. 30 North Norton Avenue, Tucson, Ariz. 85719.

UNITED STATES VOLLEYBALL ASSOCIATION. 1750 E. Boulder, Colorado Springs, Colo. 80909.

UNITED STATES YACHT RACING UNION. P.O. Box 209, Newport, R.I. 02840.

ADDENDUM

ADDENDUM

The following titles were either published subsequent to completion of the manuscript, WOMEN IN SPORT, or were not discovered in the original search for references on the subject. All titles are available from publishers in the United States.

Ammons, Pamela. SKIING FOR WOMEN. Palm Springs, Calif.: ETC Publications, 1979.

Backus, Sharron. INSIDE SOFTBALL FOR WOMEN. Chicago: Contemporary Books, 1979. Paperbound.

Barnes, Mildred J., and Kentwell, Richard G. FIELD HOCKEY: THE COACH AND THE PLAYERS. 2d ed. Rockleigh, N.J.: Allyn and Bacon, 1978.

Barthol, Robert G. PROTECT YOURSELF: A SELF DEFENSE GUIDE FOR WOMEN--FROM PREVENTION TO COUNTERATTACK. Englewood Cliffs, N.J.: Prentice-Hall, 1979.

Brown, James R., and Wardell, David. TEACHING AND COACHING GYMNASTICS FOR MEN AND WOMEN. New York: John Wiley and Sons, 1980.

Burg, Kathleen Keefe. THE WOMANLY ART OF SELF DEFENSE. Reading, Mass.: Addison-Wesley Publishing Co., 1979.

Columbu, Franco, and Columbu, Anita. STARBODIES--THE WOMEN'S WEIGHT TRAINING BOOK. New York: E.P. Dutton, 1978.

Cook, Shirley. DIARY OF A JOGGING HOUSEWIFE. Denver: Accent Books, 1978.

Covino, Marge, with Jordan, Pat. WOMAN'S GUIDE TO SHAPING YOUR BODY WITH WEIGHTS. New York: Lippincott, 1978.

Addendum

Dolan, Edward, and Lyttle, Richard B. DOROTHY HAMILL OLYMPIC SKATING. Garden City, N.Y.: Doubleday and Co., 1979.

Edmondson, Jolee. THE WOMAN GOLFER'S CATALOGUE. Briarcliff Manor, N.Y.: Stein and Day, 1979.

Englander, Joe. THEY RIDE THE RODEO: THE MEN AND WOMEN OF THE AMATEUR RODEO CIRCUIT. Riverside, N.J.: Macmillan, 1979.

Farkas, Emil, and Leeds, Margaret. FIGHT BACK: A WOMAN'S GUIDE TO SELF-DEFENSE. New York: Holt, Rinehart and Winston, 1978.

Filson, Sidney. FROM ONE WOMAN TO ANOTHER: HOW TO PROTECT YOURSELF AND SURVIVE. New York: Watts, Franklin, 1979.

Frayne, Trent. FAMOUS WOMEN TENNIS PLAYERS. New York: Dodd, Mead and Co., 1979.

Gros, Vonnie. INSIDE FIELD HOCKEY FOR WOMEN. Chicago: Contemporary Books, 1979. Paperbound.

Harrington, Anthony. EVERY GIRL'S JUDO. Buchanan, N.Y.: Emerson Books, n.d.

Hurt, Marcia. INSIDE BASKETBALL FOR WOMEN. Chicago: Contemporary Books, 1979. Paperbound.

Krementz, Jill. A VERY YOUNG SKATER. Westminster, Md.: Alfred A. Knopf, 1979.

Lighthall, Nancy. SKIING FOR WOMEN. Chicago: Chicago Review Press, 1979. Paperbound.

Lopez, Nancy, and Schwed, Peter. THE EDUCATION OF A WOMAN GOLFER. New York: Simon and Schuster, 1979.

MacDonald, Janet, and Francis, Valerie. RIDING SIDE SADDLE. Levittown, N.Y.: Transatlantic Arts, 1979.

McWhirter, Norris, et al. GUINNESS BOOK OF WOMEN'S SPORTS RECORDS. New York: Sterling Publishing Co., 1979.

Maddux, Gordon, and Shay, Arthur. FORTY COMMON ERRORS IN WOMEN'S GYMNASTICS AND HOW TO CORRECT THEM. Chicago: Contemporary Books, 1979.

Miklowitz, Gloria D. NATALIE DUNN: WORLD ROLLER SKATING CHAMPION. New York: Harcourt Brace Jovanovich, 1979.

Moffat, Gwen. SPACE BELOW MY FEET. New York: Penguin Books, 1976. Paperbound.

Murdock, Tony. GYMNASTICS FOR GIRLS. Boston: Plays, 1979.

Murray, Mimi. WOMEN'S GYMNASTICS: COACH, PARTICIPANT, SPECTATOR. Rockleigh, N.J.: Allyn and Bacon, 1979.

Peterson, Susan L. SELF-DEFENSE FOR WOMEN: THE WEST POINT WAY. New York: Simon and Schuster, 1979.

Phillips, Betty Lou. THE PICTURE STORY OF DOROTHY HAMILL. New York: Julian Messner, 1978.

Pickering, Michael G. A WOMAN'S SELF DEFENSE MANUAL. Mountain View, Calif.: World Publications, 1979.

Podesta, Terry. HOCKEY FOR MEN AND WOMEN. Boston: Charles River Books, 1978.

Steiner, Bradley J. BELOW THE BELT: UNARMED COMBAT FOR WOMEN. Thornwood, N.Y.: Paladin Enterprises, 1976.

Talbert, Peter. TRACY AUSTIN: TENNIS WONDER. East Rutherford, N.J.: G.P. Putnam's Sons, 1979.

Weckstein, Joyce R. RACQUETBALL FOR WOMEN. Royal Oak, Mich.: Lincoln Press, 1975.

Weldon, Gail. WEIGHT TRAINING FOR WOMEN'S TEAM SPORTS. Los Angeles: Weldon Publishing, 1977.

INDEXES

AUTHOR INDEX

This index includes the names of all authors, editors, and compilers cited in the text. References are to page numbers and alphabetization is letter by letter.

Author Index

TITLE INDEX

This index includes titles of all books, periodicals, and films cited in the text. Some lengthy titles have been shortened. References are to page numbers and alphabetization is letter by letter.

A

AAU News 82
Administration of Women's Competitive Sports 51
Advanced Hockey for Women 58
After Olympic Glory 20
American Fencing 82
American Woman in Sport, The 10, 15
American Women in Sports 21
Annemarie Proell 33
Approved History of the Olympic Games, An 8
Athletic and Out-Door Sports for Women 4, 15
Athletic Games in the Education of Women 3
Athletic Journal 82
Athletics in Focus 70
Athletic Training 82

B

Babe: Mildred Didrikson Zaharias 48
Babe Didrikson: The World's Greatest Woman Athlete 47
Badminton USA 82
Basic Gymnastics for Girls and Women 62

Basketball 55
Basketball--Five Players 55
Basketball for Women 56
Beginning Field Hockey 58
Below the Belt: Unarmed Combat for Women 115
Better Gymnastics for Girls 64
Better Hockey for Girls 64
Bibliography of Research Involving Female Subjects 12
Bicycling 82
Bike World 82
Billie Jean 42
Billie Jean King 37
Billie Jean King: Tennis Champion 42
Billie Jean King: The Lady of the Court 43
Book of Gymnastics, The 64
Book of Women's Achievements 23
Broken Patterns 16, 22

C

Canada's Sporting Heroes 25
Cathy Rigby: On the Beam 28
Century of Champions, A 13
Champions 19
Championship Barrel Racing 75
Championship Track and Field for Women 72

Title Index

Y

SUBJECT INDEX

This index includes major topics covered in the text. Since the entire book is concerned with women and sports, the use of woman or women with index entries has been omitted. References are to page numbers and alphabetization is letter by letter.

Subject Index

Subject Index

Subject Index